Structure Practice in Context

INTERMEDIATE  2

JAY MAURER   PENNY LAPORTE

Longman

STRUCTURE PRACTICE IN CONTEXT, Book 2

ISBN: 0 582 79859 0

First printing 1984

4 5 6 7 8 9 10–HC–95949392

Sponsoring Editor: Lyn McLean
Project Editor: Jennifer Gordon
Illustrations: Claudia Karabaic Sargent
Cover Design: Gloria J. Moyer

We wish to thank the following for providing us with photographs:

Page 42: Redwood Empire Association. **Page 47:** The University of Kansas.

Printed in the U.S.A.

Longman Inc.
1560 Broadway
New York, New York 10036

Structure Practice in Context is a series of four workbooks designed to give students practice with discrete grammar points. These points are presented in contextualized exercises so that students can see the connection between grammar and the authentic use of language.

How Is The Series Organized?

The grammar presented in the first three books consists of the grammar points that occur in the major ESL/EFL series currently available. Books One, Two and Three will complement any of the series for beginning through high-intermediate students. Book Four is for the advanced student. Here, more complex structures are introduced, with explanations not often found in books on English as a Second Language.

What Does This Series Teach Students?

Our goal as authors was to write a series that would be both structural and communicative. It is widely accepted that language acquisition is facilitated when the situation for language use is realistic and the context is meaningful. It is also clear that a structural approach, in which a single grammatical feature is presented and practiced, is effective in teaching. Grammatical accuracy is an important aspect of communicative competence. With this in mind, we have chosen to link the systematic study of grammar to the reality of communication.

What Does A Unit Look Like?

Each unit consists of one or two pages devoted to an important grammar point. The exercises progress from controlled, introductory activities to more complex tasks. We have used a variety of exercise types as well as word games to motivate students. We have also drawn on American humor, geography, history and trivia to write exercises that use language in an authentic and challenging way.

The units are ordered according to the complexity of the structure presented. Items that are generally recognized as more difficult occur later in the books. However, since each unit treats grammar points independently, there is no fixed order in which the units must be presented to the students.

How Can This Series Be Used?

The *Structure Practice in Context* workbooks can be used with a grammar-based syllabus or a notional-functional curriculum. They can be supplementary material or primary texts for independent study. We hope this series will be both useful and fun to use. We've enjoyed writing it.

TABLE OF CONTENTS

Structure Practice in Context—Book Two

PAST PROGRESSIVE

What **were you doing** at 8:00 last night?   I **was watching** T.V.
Was Jim **watching** T.V. too?   No, he **wasn't**. He **was doing** his homework.
Were Sally and Martha **doing** their homework?   No, **they weren't**. They **were making** cookies.

1. Fill in the blanks to complete the statements. Then circle *True* or *False*.

1. At 6:30 yesterday morning, the Clarks
   _____were eating_____ breakfast.
   _{eat}

(**True**) False

2. At 8:15, the children _____
   _{walk}
   to school.

True **False**

3. At 8:30, Mr. Clark _____
   _{drive}
   to work.

True **False**

4. At 9:30, Mrs. Clark _____
   _{teach}
   a class at the university.

True **False**

5. At 11:30, Mrs. Clark _____
   _{check}
   a patient at the hospital.

True **False**

6. At 8:00 P.M., Mr. and Mrs. Clark
   _____ T.V.
   _{watch}

True **False**

7. At 11:00 P.M., Mr. and Mrs. Clark
   _____ a bedtime snack.
   _{have}

True **False**

2. **Fill in the blanks. Use the past progressive form of the verbs given.**

1. POLICEMAN: Why *were you driving* so fast?
   _{you/drive}

   DRIVER: I *wasn't* . I *was* only *going* 25 miles an hour.
   _{go}

2. PRISCILLA: Why _____ about moving to Alaska?
   _{Mary/think}

   HELEN: She _____ . She _____ only _____ .
   _{joke}

3. MRS. HILL: Why _____ with your aunt?
   _{you/live}

   CHILDREN: Oh, we _____ . We _____ only _____ with her for a few weeks.
   _{stay}

4. JIM: Why _____ French in Barcelona?
   _{you/study}

   JACK: French? I _____ . I _____ Spanish.
   _{study}

3. **Fill in the blanks to complete the questions.**

A judge is asking Stan questions about his accident.

JUDGE: How fast *were you driving* ?
_{1. you/drive}

STAN: About 55 m.p.h., I think.

JUDGE: Where _____ ?
_{2. you/go}

STAN: To work.

JUDGE: And _____ ?
_{3. it/rain}

STAN: Yes, sir, it was.

JUDGE: _____ with you?
_{4. anyone/sit}

STAN: My son was in the front seat.

JUDGE: _____ a seat belt?
_{5. he/wear}

STAN: Yes, he was.

JUDGE: _____ yours?
_{6. you/wear}

STAN: No, I wasn't. I forgot.

4. **Disagree with the following statements. Use the words and phrases given.**

eat   speak   rain   sing   rest

1. A: You were sleeping.

   B: No, *I wasn't* . *I was* just *resting* my eyes.

2. A: It was snowing when we left.

   B: No, _____ . _____ just _____ .

3. A: Those people we met were speaking Portuguese.

   B: No, _____ . _____ Spanish.

4. A: That man we saw was talking to himself.

   B: No, _____ . _____ .

5. A: I was eating a carrot.

   B: No, _____ . I saw you. _____ a piece of cake!

PAST PROGRESSIVE—*As, When, While*

> We **were eating** dinner **when** the telephone **rang**.
> **When** I **woke up** yesterday, the sun **was shining**.
> **While** they **were sleeping**, the burglar **stole** their T.V.
> **As** they **were eating** dessert, the lights **went** out.

Note:

Use the past progressive to describe an **ongoing** action in the past.

Use the simple past to describe an action in the past which **happens only once**.

1. **Read the sentences. Then write the *one-time action* and the *ongoing action*.**

1. While I was making dinner, the telephone rang.
2. People were hiking up the mountain when the volcano erupted.
3. While Mr. and Mrs. Ramirez were watching T.V., a burglar broke into the house.
4. Samantha was driving down the street when her car had a flat tire.

one-time action	ongoing action
the telephone rang	*I was making dinner*

2. **Look at the picture. Write what the Thompson children *were doing* just before Mrs. Thompson returned.**

1. Nancy *was jumping* ___ on the bed.
   _{jump}
2. Bob _____ the cat.
   _{chase}
3. Andy _____ the wall.
   _{paint}
4. Jim and Johnny _____ catch.
   _{play}
5. Sarah _____ the curtains.
   _{cut}

Now write what the children *did* when they heard Mrs. Thompson come in.

6. Nancy and Bob *crawled* ___ under the bed.
   _{crawl}
7. Sarah and Jim _____ out the window.
   _{climb}
8. Andy and Johnny _____ in the closet.
   _{hide}

3. Write a simple past or past progressive verb to complete the dialogs.

1. A: When did the accident _**happen**_ ?
      <u>happen</u>
    B: While I _**was waiting**_ at the
      <u>wait</u>
      traffic light.

2. A: What happened while you _____
      _____ dinner?
      <u>make</u>
    B: My daughter _____ herself on
      <u>burn</u>
      the stove.

3. A: What happened while you _____
      _____ the movie?
      <u>watch</u>
    B: A fire _____ in the
      <u>break out</u>
      theater.

4. A: What was the thief doing when you
      _____ the gun?
      <u>see</u>
    B: He _____ out of the bank.
      <u>run</u>

5. A: What were you doing when Mom
      _____ home?
      <u>come</u>
    B: I _____ her birthday
      <u>wrap</u>
      present.

4. Fill in the blanks with simple past and past progressive forms of the verbs.

Dear Alice,

When I _**woke up**_ yesterday morning, the sun _____
  <u>1. wake up</u>   <u>2. shine</u>
and everything looked so beautiful. I _____ and
  <u>3. get up</u>
_____ my exercises. While I _____ them, the
  <u>4. do</u>   <u>5. do</u>
phone _____. It was Sandy. He _____ from the
  <u>6. ring</u>   <u>7. call</u>
airport. He _____ me to pick him up. I said OK.
  <u>8. want</u>

  While I _____, the phone _____ again.
    <u>9. get dressed</u>   <u>10. ring</u>
This time it was Mother. She _____ a ride to the dentist's. I said OK.
  <u>11. want</u>

  I _____ out the door, _____ into my car and
    <u>12. run</u>   <u>13. jump</u>
_____ off to get them. By now the sun _____
  <u>14. drive</u>   <u>15. not shine</u>
anymore. It was raining a little. As I _____ at a traffic light, another car
  <u>16. wait</u>
_____ me. It _____ my car out into the middle of
  <u>17. run into</u>   <u>18. knock</u>
the intersection. As I _____ of my car, the other driver
  <u>19. get out</u>
_____ over to me and asked me how I was. I said OK.
  <u>20. run</u>
  It was just one of those days.

                                                    Joanie

5

NOUN ADJUNCTS

What's a **house guest**?	A person who comes to visit.
What's a **guest house**?	A little house where visitors stay.
What's a **ten-story building**?	A building with ten floors.

1. **Complete the sentences.**

1. A machine that plays records is *a record player* .

2. A person who writes songs is _____ .

3. People who wash windows are _____ .

4. People who drive buses are _____ .

5. A person who paints houses is _____ .

2. **Write a sentence about each picture.**

1. *It's a ten-story building.*

2. _____

3. _____

4. They're _____

5. _____

6. _____

7. _____

8. They're _____

① building

② pole — 1 FOOT

③ flight — NEW YORK TO B | FLIGHT # | LEAVES | ARRIVES | AA 303 | 6:10 | 8:10

④ bags — GRAIN 50 LBS.

⑤ trip — LOS ANGELES / 2 Hours / SAN DIEGO

⑥ book — WAR AND PEACE

⑦ belt

⑧ tanks — 10 GALLONS PROPANE GAS

CAN and COULD—*Ability*

> I **can speak** Spanish, French and German.
> Jane **could walk** when she was ten months old.
> She **couldn't talk** until she was two years old.

1. **Match the sentences to make conversations. Write *could* or *couldn't* in the blanks.**

1. _**Could**_ you speak Spanish when you were a kid?

2. Jimmy _____ walk when he was a year old, but he couldn't talk.

3. How did you do on the geography test last Friday?

4. Did you have good seats at the football game?

5. How did you like the play?

a. No. We _____ see the players very well.

b. My Judy was just the opposite. She could talk, but she _____ walk.

c. It was great. We were in the second row, so we _____ see everything.

d. Not very well. I _____ remember the capital cities of Europe.

e. Yes, but I can't speak it very well now.

2. **Complete the conversation. Use *can, can't, could* or *couldn't*.**

Detective Drew is asking Mrs. Smith about the burglar she saw.

DETECTIVE: You say you found a burglar in the house when you got home. _**Can you remember**_ what time that was?
_{1. remember}

MRS. SMITH: Yes. It was about 10:45.

DETECTIVE: What did he look like? _____ him?
_{2. see}

MRS. SMITH: Yes, I _____ him really well. He was tall and thin.
_{3. see}

DETECTIVE: Did he say anything?

MRS. SMITH: Yes, but I _____ him very well. He spoke in a whisper.
_{4. hear}

DETECTIVE: _____ anything he said?
_{5. understand}

MRS. SMITH: I _____ a few words. He said, "Don't make any noise, lady."
_{6. understand}

DETECTIVE: Anything else?

MRS. SMITH: No, I _____ of anything right now. No, wait a minute.
_{7. think}

I _____ perfume or something. Yes, I
_{8. smell}

_____ it now. It was Sea Breeze after-shave lotion.
_{9. remember}

DETECTIVE: Sea Breeze, huh? Well, thank you, Mrs. Smith.

Aren't you coming?	Yes, I'll be right there.
Wasn't Jim here yesterday?	No, he was absent.

Note:

We use negative **yes/no** questions to show surprise, disappointment or annoyance. Negative questions show that we thought something was true, but suddenly we learn something new or different. A negative question can be answered with **yes** or **no**.

1. **Complete the questions with a negative verb. Then complete the answers. Use the words and phrases in the box.**

1. A: *Aren't* _____ bats birds?

   B: No, they're _____.

2. A: _____ Spain a republic?

   B: No, it's _____.

3. A: _____ Switzerland in World War II?

   B: No, the Swiss were _____.

4. A: _____ Madame Curie a painter?

   B: No, she was _____.

5. A: _____ the Pharaohs Turks?

   B: No, they were _____.

Egyptians
a kingdom
mammals
neutral
a scientist

2. **Complete the questions with a negative verb. Then complete the answers with *Yes* or *No*.**

Frank and Stan are at the office Christmas party.

FRANK: Look. There's Janice Carter.

STAN: *Isn't* _____ she Mr. Griswold's private secretary? [1]

FRANK: No, why?

STAN: I thought she was. She's always in his office. Where is he, anyway? And where's Sylvia? _____ they here yet? [2]

FRANK: _____, they're going to be late. [3]

STAN: Hey, I'm starving. _____ you? [4] _____ there any food here? [5]

FRANK: _____, there is. It's in the other room. Let's check it out. [6]

STAN: Um, you go ahead.

FRANK: _____ you coming? I thought you were hungry. [7]

STAN: _____, I'm going to stay here a minute. Do you see the woman at the door? [8] _____ she beautiful? [9]

FRANK: _____, she is. She's my girlfriend. [10]

STAN: Oh.

> **Can't** you understand me?
> **Couldn't** you remember the answers?
>
> Yes, I can, but you speak fast.
> No. I was too sleepy.

Note:

We generally use negative questions to show surprise, disappointment or annoyance.

1. **Fill in the blanks to complete the advertisement. Use *can't* and a subject.**

Get *SLEEPIES* and Get to Sleep

What's the matter? *Can't you* get to sleep? Your neighbors always have a fight at 3 A.M., don't they? _____ ever be quiet?
2

And your six-year-old son always wants one more glass of water. _____ get through one
3

night without waking up? You had a busy day at work, but everything is OK. _____
4

relax and forget about work? And that's not all! Your husband tosses and turns in his sleep.

_____ be still for once?
5

Here's the answer to all your problems. Get **Sleepies**, the safe, fast way to a peaceful night. No more noise. No more tossing. Get **Sleepies** and sleep, sleep, sleep.

2. **Complete the sentences with *can't* or *couldn't*.**

1. MAN: Driver, *can't* you go any faster? I'm going to miss my plane.

   DRIVER: Take it easy. I'm doing the best I can.

2. DIANE: _____ Jim come skiing with us this weekend?

   MARIA: No. He has too much work to do.

   DIANE: Oh, that's too bad.

3. VINCE: I don't think I passed the exam.

   PHIL: _____ you understand it?

   VINCE: Yeah, but I didn't finish.

4. SALLY: I had a terrible time getting around in Italy.

   JULIA: Why? _____ you ask for help?

   SALLY: Yes, but no one understood my Italian.

NEGATIVE QUESTIONS—*Do*

Don't you like wine?	No, I hate it.
Doesn't it ever rain here?	Yes, it rains a lot in the winter.
Didn't you deposit your check?	No, I forgot.

1. **Match the sentences to make conversations. Fill in the blanks with *don't*, *doesn't* or *didn't* and a subject if necessary.**

1. *Doesn't it* _____ ever snow here?

2. _____ invite Lucy?

3. _____ have a savings account?

4. _____ tell you about Mary?

5. _____ the Martinsons eat meat?

6. _____ get my letter?

a. No. I only invited Melanie.

b. No. I didn't get any letters today.

c. Sure. It snows in February and March.

d. No. I don't have any savings!

e. No. You just told me about Susan.

f. No. They're vegetarians.

2. **Complete the questions. Use *don't* or *didn't* and a subject.**

STAN: Honey, where's my shirt? *Didn't you*₁ _____ wash it?

MARCIA: Sure, it's in the closet. _____₂_____ see it?

STAN: No, I don't. . . . Oh, there it is, but it's wrinkled. _____₃_____ iron it?

MARCIA: Oh, gee, I forgot. Sorry. Is there something else you can wear?

STAN: No, nothing's clean. Marcia, I'm tired of wearing wrinkled shirts. _____₄_____ love me any more?

MARCIA: Of course I do, Stan, but I'm so busy. _____₅_____ know how to iron?

STAN: That's not the point.

3. **Write negative verbs to complete the questions. Then complete the answers. Use the words and phrases given.**

1. A: *Don't* _____ tigers live in Africa?

    B: No, they *live* _____ in *Asia* _____.

2. A: _____ a Mercedes cost a lot?

    B: Yes, it _____.

3. A: _____ World War II start in 1938?

    B: No, it _____ in _____.

Asia
1939
over $15,000

CAN and COULD—Requests and Permission

> Asking for permission:
> Mom, **can I** have an ice cream cone? No, **you can't**. It's almost dinnertime.
>
> Requesting:
> Mrs. Cole, **could I** see you for a moment? Yes, of course.

Note:

Could is sometimes considered a more formal or polite way of asking permission or making a request.

1. Complete the conversation. Use *can* and a pronoun.

JULIE: Mom, *can I*___ invite Katy for the weekend?
         ⎯1⎯

MOTHER: I guess so. Did Katy ask her mother?

JULIE: Yes, she did. _____ come for dinner?
                          2

MOTHER: Yes, I guess so.

JULIE: _____ go to the movies after dinner?
            3

MOTHER: Do you and Katy have enough money?

JULIE: Yes, plenty. _____ go?
                         4

MOTHER: I suppose you can, but you have to be home by 10:00.

JULIE: Mom, _____ invite Pam too?
                 5

MOTHER: Oh, Julie, that's too many people.

JULIE: All right, Mom, just Katy. _____ stay up late and watch T.V.? I mean after we
                                       6
         get home.

MOTHER: Well, OK. Tomorrow's Saturday.

JULIE: One more thing. _____ go swimming tomorrow?
                            7

MOTHER: All three of you? Well, all right. Now go and set the table.

2. Match the sentences.

1. Hey, Pete. Can you come here a second?

2. I'm sorry to bother you, but could you reach that box up there for me?

3. Can I come in?

4. Miss Gilbert, could I see you in my office?

a. Of course, Mr. Kline. I'll be right in.

b. OK. Just a minute.

c. Sure. The door's open.

d. Certainly. I'd be glad to.

11

INFINITIVE STRUCTURES—*Verb + Infinitive*

> Mary **wants to be** a doctor.
> She **doesn't want to be** a nurse.
>
> **Does** she **need to know** chemistry?

1. **Complete the sentences with the correct forms of the verbs.**

Terry Fox was a remarkable young man. He had a serious disease—cancer. The cancer was in his right leg so the doctors _wanted to save_ Terry's life by amputating that leg.
_{1. want/save}

Terry _____ the operation. When it was over, he had only one leg, but
_{2. agree/have}

he _____ sorry about it. Instead, he _____
_{3. refuse/feel} _{4. decide/do}

something important. He _____ across Canada. This way he
_{5. plan/run}

_____ money for cancer research. He _____
_{6. hope/raise} _{7. promise/continue}

fighting against the disease as long as he could. People from all over the world _____

_____ his fight. When Terry died, he had almost achieved
_{8. offer/support}

his dream. His example has given courage and strength to many others.

2. **Complete the questions.**

1. A: _Does_ a chemistry teacher _need to_ know algebra?
   _{need}
   B: Yes, algebra is really helpful.

2. A: _____ a doctor _____ study chemistry?
   _{have}
   B: Yes, chemistry is essential.

3. A: _____ teachers _____ correct papers?
   _{like}
   B: No, they usually hate it.

4. A: _____ a teacher _____ have a college degree?
   _{have}
   B: Yes, a college degree is a requirement.

5. A: _____ you _____ speak English fluently?
   _{want}
   B: Yes, it's a must for an interpreter.

6. A: _____ an editor _____ be a good speller?
   _{have}
   B: Yes. She also needs a good dictionary.

3. Write sentences about yourself. Use *like to* and *don't like to*. You can use the suggestions in the pictures below.

cook

drive

play the guitar

stay up late

dance

get up early

roller skate

study

do housework

meet new people

ski

swim

like to	don't like to
1. *I like to go dancing.*	6.
2. *I don't like to cook.*	7.
3.	8.
4.	9.
5.	10.

INFINITIVE STRUCTURES—Verb + Object + Infinitive

> The teacher **wants the students to listen.**
> She **doesn't want them to talk.**

1. **The Bradley children have jobs to do. Look at the chart. Then fill in the blanks with an *infinitive*.**

> 1. Do the dishes – Sam + Nancy
> 2. Mow the lawn – Sam
> 3. Clean up the livingroom – Sam + Nancy
> 4. Do grocery shopping – Nancy
> 5. Make beds – Dave
> 6. Wash windows – Nancy
> 7. Pick up clothes – Sam + Dave
> 8. Feed dog – Sam

1. Mrs. Bradley wants Sam and Nancy

   _to do_ the dishes.
   (do)

2. She asked Sam _____ the lawn.
   (mow)

3. She told all three of them

   _____ the living room.
   (clean up)

4. She wanted Nancy _____

   the shopping.
   (do)

5. She asked Dave _____ the beds.
   (make)

6. She told Nancy _____ the windows.
   (wash)

7. She ordered the boys _____

   their clothes immediately.
   (pick up)

8. She asked Sam _____ the dog.
   (feed)

2. **Nancy didn't do her tasks and Mrs. Bradley is angry. Write sentences about what *she told her to do* and *didn't tell her to do*.**

1. _She told her to_ _____ do the dishes.

2. _She didn't tell her to_ _____ read a book.

3. _____ clean up the living room.

4. _____ watch television.

5. _____ wash the windows.

6. _____ listen to the radio.

7. _____ do the shopping.

8. _____ take a bath.

3. Complete the conversation. Use infinitive structures.

HELEN: What *do you want me to do* first?
                                     1. want/do

MR. STEEL: Why don't you call Mr. Kramer?

HELEN: All right. Then _____ those reports?
                                    2. want/type

MR. STEEL: No, not yet. Go talk to Mrs. Brady. She _____ some things

                                              3. want/do

               for her this morning.

HELEN: Oh. What does she need?

MR. STEEL: She'd _____ some letters. Also, be sure you
                             4. like/type

               _____ the Sperry account.
                        5. ask/check

HELEN: OK.

MR. STEEL: Oh, and Helen, when you see Frank, _____ here, please.
                                                     6. ask/come in

               I _____ me with something.
                      7. want/help

4. Unscramble the sentences.

Tony	Janice
1. dinner you ask the did Millers to to come ?	**2.** tonight yes, them I asked come to

TONY: *Did you ask the Millers to come to dinner?*
                                        1

JANICE: _____
                        2
          _____

Scott	Karen
3. Alice me does party to to want come the ?	**4.** she you come to of course wants

SCOTT: _____
                       3
        _____

KAREN: _____
                       4
        _____

Are you going to the bank today? No, I don't **need to**.	Don't you ever watch T.V.? No, I don't **like to**.
Is Sally bringing the dessert? No. I didn't **ask her to**.	Did you study for the test? No, and I don't **have to**.
Dave didn't write to his parents. He will. I'll **tell him to**.	Frank, it's time to do the dishes. Oh, Dad. I don't **want to** right now.

1. **Match the sentences to make conversations. Fill in the blanks with *want to, need to, like to* or *have to*.**

1. Why are you walking to work?
2. Don't you ever dance?
3. Why doesn't Sally marry Bill?
4. Why is Fred taking this class?

a. She doesn't _____. He's poor.
b. I _**have to**_. Dad has the car keys.
c. No, I don't _____ dance.
d. He _____ for his M.A. degree.

2. **Complete the dialogs.**

1. A: Is Bobby going to come to the party?
   B: I don't know. I _**asked him to**_ .
   _{ask}
2. A: Did Betty feed the dog?
   B: I hope so. I _____.
   _{tell}
3. A: Is your daughter going to marry Frank?
   B: I hope not. I _____ really _____.
   _(negative) _{want}
4. A: Did Dave come to visit you in Mexico?
   B: No. I _____ really _____. I wanted to be alone.
   _(negative) _{want}
5. A: Are the Petersons bringing their children?
   B: I don't think so. I _____, but Jenny has a cold.
   _{ask}
6. A: Why didn't Bobby lock the door?
   B: I _____. It's not his fault.
   _{(negative) tell}

> What kind of employee is Angela?
>
> She's an excellent employee.
> She works **hard**. She types **fast**. She gets along **well** with everyone.

1. Complete the conversations. Use *well, hard* or *fast*.

1. A: Do you want Harry to do this job?

    B: Yes. He works *hard*, and he's smart too.

2. A: I need this report done right away. Who can I get?

    B: What about Roger? He types really _____.

3. A: I need some help with my Spanish.

    B: Try Julia. She speaks Spanish very _____.

4. A: Do you want to take the bus?

    B: No, I want to find a taxi. I have to get there _____.

5. A: How did I do on the test?

    B: Very _____. You got 98%.

6. A: How do you feel today?

    B: Tired. I worked _____ yesterday.

2. Complete the questions. Use *how fast, how hard* or *how well*.

1. BOSS: Do you want the job?

    JACK: I don't know. *How hard* do I have to work?

2. ROGER: _____ did Sam run in the race?

    MARY: He did the first mile in five minutes.

3. BOSS: Do you have anyone you can recommend for a secretarial job?

    AGENCY: I think so, but _____ does the person have to type?

4. BEN: _____ can Mary speak Spanish?

    JAIME: Very well. Why?

    BEN: Here's a job as an interpreter.

5. MR. BROWN: Do you want to give this project to John Davidson?

    MR. LUCAS: I don't know. _____ does he work?

    MR. BROWN: He's a very hard worker.

VERY and TOO

> That car is **very** expensive, but I think we can afford it.
> That car is **too** expensive. We can't afford it.
>
> I don't like big cities. There's **too much** pollution. And there are **too many** people.

1. Fill in the blanks with *very* and an adjective from the list.

small   tall   big   old   young   short   cheap   expensive

1. Barkerville is a _very small_ town.
2. Tokyo is a _____ city.

3. Ahmed Rashid is a _____ man.
4. Joe Jenkins is a _____ man.

5. Mary Clinger is _____.
6. Jimmy Banks is _____.

7. This Cadillac is _____.
8. This Chevrolet is _____.

2. Match the sentences to make conversations. Write *too* and one of the words given.

expensive   many   much   nice   short   sweet

1. Let's go to the movies.
2. Do you think we can get Billy that racing bicycle for his birthday?
3. Did you do your homework?
4. Don't you think Harold is a nice person?
5. Do you want some cake?
6. If you need a job, why don't you go into police work?

a. I'm _____. I'm only 5 feet.
b. No, I ate _too much_. I can't move.
c. Thanks, but I don't like cake. It's _____.
d. Not yet. It has _____ problems.
e. He's just a little _____.
f. I don't think so. It's _____ for our budget.

3. Complete the dialogs with *very* or *too* and an adjective. Use *fast*, *late* or *expensive*.

1. ALICE: What about the new car? Can we get it?

   PETER: Not this year. It's _too expensive_ .

2. SAM: Well, are we going to buy the house or not?

   PAT: It's _____, but I think we can afford it.

3. BOB: Are we going to get to the game by 8:00?

   BERT: Well, it's _____, but I think we can get there on time.

4. SALLY: Let's go. We're going to miss the movie if we don't hurry.

   JUAN: Forget it. It's _____ now. It starts in five minutes.

5. BILL: Do you think you can beat Stan in the race?

   HANK: Well, he's _____, but I think I can win.

6. HELEN: Why don't you enter the race? You can win.

   BECKY: No, not this year. Amy is _____. I can't beat her.

4. Fill in the blanks with *too much*, *too many* or *very*.

Dear Mom and Dad,

I'm in New York City. I'm _very_₁ happy to be here, but I'm a little tired too. For some people there is ___₂___ noise and ___₃___ people in this city. Well, not for me. I think the life style is ___₄___ exciting. I'll be here one week and then I'll go to Pennsylvania and Washington, D.C. After that, I'll be in Canada, if it doesn't cost ___₅___. There are ___₆___ stories and adventures to write down. I'll tell you everything when I get home.

Wish you were here. Give Scotty a ___₇___ big hug for me.

Love,

Pam

19

ADVERBS and HOW

> **How** is Sally doing in English?
> Pretty **well**. She does her work **quickly** and **carefully**.

Note:

For adjectives ending in **y**, change the **y** to **i** and add **-ly**.

   happy → **happily**

For adjectives ending in **e**, drop the **e** and add **-ly**.

   terrible → **terribly**

For adjectives ending in **l**, simply add **-ly**.

   careful → **carefully**

Remember: Irregular adverbs like **well**, **hard** and **fast** do not end in **-ly**.

1. Look at the pictures and say how each person *is doing* or *did* the action. Use the words given and add *-ly*.

bad   careful   careless   happy   quick   sad   slow   good

1. Mike is driving *Carelessly* _____ .

2. Rhoda is driving very _____ .

3. Hank did the dishes _____ .

4. Wilma did the dishes _____ .

5. Helen answered _____ .

6. Jeff answered _____ .

7. Sarah did _____ on the test.

8. Ray did _____ on the test.

2. Complete the conversations with *how* and adverbs.

1. A: How about Tom Sill for the bus driver job?

   B: I don't know. *How well does he drive* ?
                good/drive

   A: *Very well and very carefully* .
           good/careful

2. A: What about Amy for the secretarial job?

   B: I don't know. _____ ?
               fast/type

   A: _____ .
         fast/accurate

3. A: What about Jason for the writing job?

   B: I don't know. _____ ?
               good/write

   A: _____ .
         good/quick

4. A: How about Kim for our translator?

   B: _____ ?
       fluent/speak Russian

   A: _____ .
       fluent

3. **Fill in the blanks to complete the letter. Remember that *hard*, *fast* and *good* have irregular adverb forms.**

The Jensen family recently moved to Los Angeles.

> 3688 Rosemont Circle
> Los Angeles, California
>
> Dear Helen,
>
> We finally got settled in our new house and things are going _____*well*_____. The movers
> 1. good
>
> came yesterday and moved all the furniture in really _____. But whenever you deal with
> 2. fast
>
> movers, there's always one who doesn't work _____. One guy dropped our T.V. set. I
> 3. careful
>
> reacted pretty _____, I think. I yelled at him a lot. Then the chief mover said the
> 4. bad
>
> company will _____ pay for the damages, so I felt better.
> 5. glad
>
> Stan likes his new job, but he's already working _____. The kids started school last
> 6. hard
>
> week—Betty _____ and Jim not so _____.
> 7. eager   8. eager
>
> How are things with you folks? We miss you all _____. Thanks for the goodbye
> 9. terrible
>
> party you had for us. You plan parties so _____.
> 10. good
>
> I have to stop now because it's dinner time and I need to get dinner ready _____. If I
> 11. quick
>
> don't, I'll have three starving people. Write soon.
>
> Love, *Amanda*

4. **Unscramble the sentences.**

1. A: you test did the on well do?

   Did you do well on the test?

   B: no, terribly did I.

2. A: into garage the slowly very drove Sara.

   B: she my bicycle over ran.

3. A: husband Doctor, is doing my how?

   B: resting he's comfortably.

4. A: beautifully play you.

   B: I it enjoy.

5. A: English speaks she fluently.

   B: hard very studies she.

> Word order with nouns:
>
> Let's go to the movies.
> I can't. I don't have **enough money**.
>
> Word order with adjectives:
>
> Michele wants to be a ballerina.
> Good. She's still **young enough** to do it.

1. Read the situations. Then write questions with *enough* and answer them.

Situation 1: Willy wants to buy a new bicycle which costs $80. He saved $40, and his father gave him $30.

Does he have enough money? *No* .

Situation 2: It's 4:45 and Rebecca's plane leaves at 5:15. It takes an hour to get to the airport.

_____ time? _____.

Situation 3: It's 8:20 and Ben has to be at work by 9 o'clock. It takes half an hour to get there.

_____ time? _____.

Situation 4: Mrs. Brandon has one gallon of milk. She needs three quarts for her family, one quart for the cat and one quart for the soup she's making.

_____ milk? _____.

2. Complete the sentences. Use *enough* and one of the words given.

good   long   patience   smart   space

1. A: Is Jim going to college next year?

   B: No, his grades aren't *good enough* .

2. A: Do you think Mary is going to be a lawyer?

   B: Well, she's certainly _____ to be one.

3. A: Why don't you become an elementary school teacher?

   B: I don't have _____ .

4. A: What's wrong with my English paper, Mr. Gomez?

   B: It's just not _____. You need to write more.

5. A: Why are you moving to the country?

   B: The city is too crowded. I don't have _____ .

TOO and ENOUGH

> Can we go to the movies?
> No, it's **too** late now. We don't have **enough** time to get there.
>
> Do we have **enough** time to make it to Philadelphia by 8:00?
> No. It's **too** far.

1. **Fill in the blanks with *too* or *enough* to complete the conversation.**

WENDY: I'm _____*too*_____ fat.
$_1$

JANE: Well, go on a diet.

WENDY: I don't have _____ patience to stay on a diet. I'm so fat that nobody likes me.
$_2$

JANE: Wendy, that's not true.

WENDY: It *is* true. Everybody thinks I'm _____ boring to be any fun. I don't have
$_3$

_____ money to live on either.
$_4$

JANE: Why don't you try to get a better job?

WENDY: I don't have _____ skills and I'm _____ ugly. I can't get another job.
$_5$ $_6$

JANE: Wendy, do you know what your problem is? You're _____ pessimistic. You don't have
$_7$

_____ confidence in yourself.
$_8$

2. **Read the advertisement for Oaties, a new cereal. Then complete the sentences with *too* or *enough* and one of the words given.**

time   rushed   much   tired   energy   late

ANNOUNCER: What's the matter? _____*Too tired*_____
$_1$

to work? Not _____
$_2$

_____ to finish the job?

MAGGIE: That's right. I'm exhausted!

ANNOUNCER: You probably got up _____
$_3$

to have a good breakfast.

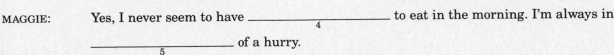

MAGGIE: Yes, I never seem to have _____ to eat in the morning. I'm always in
$_4$

_____ of a hurry.
$_5$

ANNOUNCER: Well, why don't you try Oaties? It's a new nutritious oat cereal.

MAGGIE: I told you. I'm _____ in the morning to eat!
$_6$

ANNOUNCER: Not any more. Oaties are *bars* of cereal! You can eat them anywhere!

23

COMBINING FORMS—*Some, Any, Every, No*

Some- somebody, someone, something, somewhere, sometime

I want to do **something** interesting this weekend.

Any- anybody, anyone, anything, anywhere, anytime

I didn't go **anywhere** last weekend.

No- nobody, no one, nothing, nowhere

Nobody came to see me.

Every- everybody, everyone, everything, everywhere, every time

Everyone was out of town.

---

1. **Complete the dialogs. Use words from the grammar box above.**

1. A: What did you do this weekend?

   B: _**Nothing**_. I stayed home and slept.

2. A: How many of your students are here today?

   B: _____ is. Nobody's absent for the third day in a row.

3. A: Where did you go after the movie?

   B: _____. We went home early and watched T.V. for a while.

4. A: Who did you go to the movies with?

   B: _____. I went alone.

5. A: Did you go somewhere on Saturday?

   B: No, we didn't go _____.

6. A: Where did you look for your ring?

   B: _____. There's no place I *didn't* look.

2. **Complete the letter. Use words from the grammar box.**

Dear Dad,

**Everything** is fine here at school. My roommate is a guy from _____
$\quad$ 1 $\qquad\qquad\qquad\qquad\qquad\qquad\qquad\qquad\qquad\qquad$ 2

in Alabama—he's OK. Last week we went _____ every night, but this week we
$\qquad\qquad\qquad\qquad\qquad\qquad\qquad$ 3

have to study, so we can't go _____. I know almost _____ on my
$\qquad\qquad\qquad\qquad$ 4 $\qquad\qquad\qquad\qquad\qquad\qquad$ 5

floor, but I don't know _____ on the other floors. There's homework for every
$\qquad\qquad\qquad\qquad\qquad$ 6

class. The teachers all give us _____ to do every night.
$\qquad\qquad\qquad\qquad\qquad\qquad$ 7

Did I say _____ is fine here? Not quite. I left my bicycle by the library, and
$\qquad\qquad\qquad$ 8

_____ stole it. The campus police say there's probably _____ they
$\qquad$ 9 $\qquad\qquad\qquad\qquad\qquad\qquad\qquad$ 10

can do about it. Now _____ I see _____ on a red bicycle with a
$\qquad\qquad$ 11 $\qquad\qquad\qquad\qquad$ 12

black basket I wonder if it's my bike.

Call me _____ you want to. I'm always here. On second thought, I'll call you
$\qquad$ 13

_____ on Sunday. OK?
$\quad$ 14

$\qquad\qquad\qquad\qquad\qquad\qquad\qquad\qquad$ Love, *Luke*

---

3. **Make statements about the pictures. Use words from the grammar box.**

1. There are eight students in Mrs. Adams'

   class. _Everyone_ is here today.

   Yesterday, _____ was absent,

   but I'm not sure who it was.

2. Right now, Mr. Stevens isn't doing

   _____ .

   Now Mr. Stevens is doing _____ ,

   but *what*?

4. **Complete the crossword puzzle.**

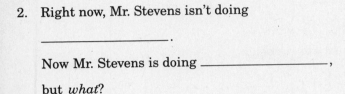

| ¹N | O | ²W | ³H | ⁴E | ⁵R | E |

Across

1. in no location
6. I _____ two sisters and one brother.
7. My brother is _____ tall as I am.
9. Is any_____ home?
10. Nickname for Edward
12. Philadelphia is the four___ largest city in the United States.
13. I looked _____ for my wallet.
14. _____ everyone ready to go?
16. _____ of the students failed the test. All of the scores were above 70%.
17. location
19. you and I
20. nickname for Alan
21. Isn't _____ coming with me?

Down

1. no person
2. Did you go any_____ last night?
3. ha, _____
4. _____ is here. No one is absent.
5. the color of blood
8. Jim wants to marry _____ who is kind.
11. _____ pictures are beautiful. Those are ugly.
12. "What did you do last night?" No_____."
15. Sick
17. You can cook fish in a _____ .
18. _____ you speak Spanish?
19. method

25

PRESENT PERFECT SIMPLE—*Ever, Never, Lately, Recently*

> **Have you done** anything interesting **recently?**
> **lately?**
> Yes, **I ran** in a race last weekend.
>
> **Have you ever been** to Montreal?
> No, **I haven't**, but **I've been** to Toronto. I **was there** last summer.
> How about Niagara Falls?
> No, **I've never been there** either.

1. **Fill in the blanks with the present perfect form of the verbs given.**

Officer Bartoli is talking to Dave Denton about a crime.

OFFICER: *Have you ever been* in trouble, Mr. Denton?
　　　　　 1. you/ever be

DAVE: Uh, yes, but that was a long time ago. I *haven't done* anything lately.
　　　　　　　　　　　　　　　　　　　　　　　　　　　 2. not do

OFFICER: Really? Our records show that _____ in trouble recently.
　　　　　　　　　　　　　　　　　　　　　　　 3. you/be

DAVE: Well, uh, yes, but I _____ back to jail.
　　　　　　　　　　　　　　 4. never go

OFFICER: _____ your old partner Mugsy recently?
　　　　　　 5. you/see

DAVE: No. I haven't.

OFFICER: _____ a black Cadillac, Mr. Denton?
　　　　　 6. you/ever drive

DAVE: No, I _____. Absolutely not!
　　　　　　　　　　 7

OFFICER: I hope you can prove that, Mr. Denton. The black Cadillac was involved in a serious crime. So was Mugsy. And we know that Mugsy can't drive.

2. **Fill in the blanks to complete the conversations. Use *never* and the present perfect.**

1. A: What's Ruth like?

   B: I don't know. *I've never met her.*
   　　　　　　　　　　 I/never meet her

2. A: Is Portland an interesting city?

   B: I couldn't say. _____
   　　　　　　　　　　　　 I/never be there

3. A: Does Julie approve of your plan?

   B: Who knows? _____
   　　　　　　　　　 we/never talk about it

4. A: What's it like to fly in an airplane?

   B: I have no idea. _____
   　　　　　　　　　　　 I/never fly in one

5. A: Is my idea good?

   B: How do I know? _____
   　　　　　　　　　　　 you/never discuss it with me

3. Complete the dialogs with the present perfect.

1. A: _Have you seen_ any good movies lately?
      _{you/see}

   B: Yes. We saw *Star Wars* last Thursday.

2. A: _____ *War and Peace*?
      _{you/ever read}

   B: Yeah, we had to read it in high school.

3. A: Jason, _____ me a lie?
      _{you/ever tell}

   B: No. I _____ anyone a lie.
      _{never/tell}

4. A: _____ a day's work in his life?
      _{Don/ever do}

   B: I don't think so. He's as lazy as they come.

5. A: The kids look tired. _____?
      _{they/eat}

   B: Yes. We all ate before we came.

4. Write sentences using the present perfect and the past tense. Look at the chart.

Kenyon College Alumnae Update—Class of 1960

Sacks, Samuel—Poet
2 poems—
<u>Electra</u> in April
<u>Songs of Life</u> in May

Smith, Alice—Runner
6 races—
First place in the
   Boston Marathon, May

Svartvik, Eli—Film director
2 short films—
<u>Bombay</u>—January
<u>The Last World</u>—May

Santana, Luis—Civic leader
2 awards—
the Outstanding Citizen
   of Wobegon
the R. C. Fields Award

Stone, Bill and Gladys—Retired
3 safaris—
Kenya in January
Ethiopia in February
India in April

---

1. Sam Sacks
   (write/publish/recently)
   has written two poems recently. He published Electra in April and Songs of Life in May.

2. Luis Santana
   (receive/get/recently)
   _____

3. Alice Smith
   (run/take/in the past three months)
   _____

4. Bill and Gladys Stone
   (go on/be/recently)
   _____

5. Eli Svartvik
   (make/finish/in the past six months)
   _____

How long have you **been** married? **For** 10 years. / **Since** 1978. / Ten years.
I got married in 1978.   OR   **I have been** / **I've been** married **since** 1978.
Carlos moved to Canada 19 years ago.   OR   He **has** / He**'s** lived in Canada **for** 19 years.

Note:

Use **for** with *quantities* of time.

Use **since** with *points* in time.

1. Use *for* or *since* in the sentences.

1. A: Have you practiced your piano today?

   B: Yeah.

   A: How long?

   B: Come on, Mom. *For* at least an hour.

2. A: Have you lived here long?

   B: Oh, yes. _____ 1963.

3. A: How long have they had their summer home?

   B: _____ a few years. They bought it when they retired.

4. A: Have you been skiing recently?

   B: No, not _____ last winter.

2. Fill in the blanks. Use the correct form of the verb.

THE COUPLES GAME
COUPLE #1 — TIM AND CAROLYN CLARK

1976	met in San Antonio	1980	Carolyn got a job with an insurance company
1977	got married	1982	Bought first house
1978	moved to Dallas	1983	First child, Kimberly, born
1979	Tim got a job as an architect		

Meet couple number one—Tim and Carolyn Clark. Tim and Carolyn *have known* each other for eight years

in all. They _____ married in 1977. They
        2. get

_____ in Dallas since 1977. Tim _____ as an architect for five
    3. live   4. work

years, and Carolyn _____ for an insurance company for four. They _____
                5. work   6. be

homeowners since 1980. They _____ their first child, Kimberly, in 1983.
                    7. have

Now let's see what Tim and Carolyn may win today.

3. **Write questions using the present perfect.**

Peter Bond hopes to get a loan from First National Bank of Gainesville.

LOAN OFFICER: <u>How long have you been married</u>, Mr. Bond?
1. be married

PETER BOND: Well, Helen and I got married in 1971—so that's 13 years.

LOAN OFFICER: You're at Ace Instruments now, I see.

_____ there?
2. work

PETER BOND: Let's see . . . since 1973.

LOAN OFFICER: And your wife teaches at Lincoln High School.

_____ there?
3. teach

PETER BOND: Just two years.

LOAN OFFICER: OK. Now, you have a house at 660 Madison Circle.

_____ in that house?
4. live

PETER BOND: Five years.

LOAN OFFICER: _____ the house for five years?
5. own

PETER BOND: No, we rented for the first three.

LOAN OFFICER: Thank you, Mr. Bond. Your application looks good.

4. **It is 1984. Write sentences with *for* or *since* and the present perfect.**

Frank Silvers moved to Toronto in 1973. For several months he couldn't find a job, but in 1974 he got a teaching position at Minnetonka Elementary School. In 1975, he met Susan Miller. They got married in 1978. In 1980, Frank became principal of Minnetonka. Frank and Susan bought a house in 1981, and in 1983 they bought five acres of land in the country.

1. <u>Frank has lived in Toronto since 1973 / for 11 years.</u>
Frank/live in Toronto

2. _____
he/work at Minnetonka Elementary School

3. _____
he/be principal of the school

4. _____
Frank and Susan/know each other

5. _____
they/be married

6. _____
they/have their house

7. _____
they/own their property in the country

What **have you been doing** lately?
I**'ve seen** a few good movies and **gone** to a couple of concerts.

I**'ve been living** here for almost two months.

My wife **has been working** at the hospital since December.
She**'s** also **been writing** a book in her spare time.

Note:

The present perfect and the present perfect progressive are often interchangeable. However, in some cases the progressive shows that an action is not yet finished.
My wife has been writing a book means that she *has not yet finished the book*.
My wife has written a book means that she *has finished the book*.

1. **Jim and Lorraine Hardy recently moved to Milwaukee. Complete the sentences about what they have been doing since then. Use the present perfect progressive.**

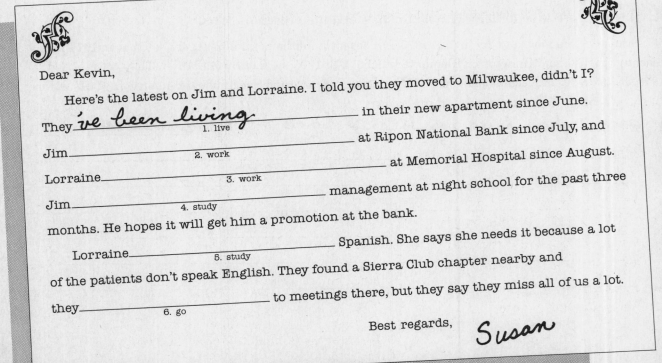

Dear Kevin,

    Here's the latest on Jim and Lorraine. I told you they moved to Milwaukee, didn't I?

They *'ve been living* _____ in their new apartment since June.
         1. live

Jim _____ at Ripon National Bank since July, and
      2. work

Lorraine _____ at Memorial Hospital since August.
        3. work

Jim _____ management at night school for the past three
    4. study

months. He hopes it will get him a promotion at the bank.

    Lorraine _____ Spanish. She says she needs it because a lot
          5. study

of the patients don't speak English. They found a Sierra Club chapter nearby and

they _____ to meetings there, but they say they miss all of us a lot.
    6. go

             Best regards,

                Susan

2. Fill in the blanks with a present perfect progressive to complete the dialogs.

1. A: How long _have you been smoking_ (you/smoke) ?

   B: Two years, but I want to quit.

2. A: How long _____ (she/wear) contact lenses?

   B: Just a month. She went to the optician in May.

3. A: What _____ (you/do) lately?

   B: Well, I got married last month.

4. A: How long _____ (Jim and Nancy/date)?

   B: Since they met—in August.

5. A: How long _____ (she/play) the guitar?

   B: For two years. She played the piano before that.

6. A: How long _____ (we/talk)?

   B: Oh, several hours. But we've had a lot to talk about.

3. Complete the sentences with a present perfect progressive.

1. John Jones is a writer. He's written two books, and _he's been writing_ a third since last November.

2. Linda has read ten books already this year, and _____ this one for the last week.

3. Ace Building Company has constructed eleven buildings in three years. They _____ _____ this one since right after Christmas.

4. Michael has painted many pictures over the past few years. He _____ this new one for a month or so.

5. Mrs. Appleby has made four dresses in the last three months. _____ this fifth one for a week.

6. The students have taken five tests already this week. _____ this extra one for the last hour.

7. Mr. Mason has built five houses in the last year, and _____ this other one for the past two months.

8. Anne Stone has typed five reports already today, and _____ the sixth one since 3 o'clock.

31

PRESENT PERFECT—Indefinite Time Expressions

> What **have you seen since you got here**?
>
> Well, I**'ve been** to the Empire State Building and the Metropolitan Museum. I **haven't seen** a Broadway play **yet**.
>
> **Has he enjoyed** his stay in New York **so far**?
> Yes. He really likes it here.

1. Jerry Anderson is in New York City for a week. Look at the chart. Write sentences about what he has and hasn't done *so far*.

1. *He has climbed the Statue of Liberty.*
2. *He hasn't visited the World Trade Center.*
3. _____
4. _____
5. _____
6. _____
7. _____
8. _____

Climb the Statue of Liberty ✔
Visit the World Trade Center
See a Broadway play
eat in Greenwich Village ✔
visit the United Nations ✔
go to Central Park
go shopping at Macy's ✔
ride the subways

2. Complete the dialogs with the present perfect.

1. A: *Has Jim finished* _____ his
      (Jim/finish)
   term paper on the Civil War yet?

   B: No, not yet. It's due on Friday.

2. A: _____
         (Robin/get out of)
   the hospital yet?

   B: No, she doesn't leave until Monday.

3. A: Billy, _____ your
            (you/do)
   homework for math class?

   B: No, but I'm going to start soon.

4. A: _____ your house yet?
         (you/sell)

   B: No, but I think I have a buyer.

5. A: _____ through
         (we/go)
   Pennsylvania yet?

   B: Are you kidding? We haven't even gotten through Ohio.

6. A: What _____ so far
              (you/see)
   during your stay in Los Angeles?

   B: Well, we've been to Disneyland and Knotts Berry Farm. And we saw a movie studio.

3. Complete the conversations with the present perfect.

1. A: Let's not hire Mr. Appleby. He hasn't had any teaching experience.

   B: That's true, but _he's had administrative experience_ .
   administrative experience

2. A: I like your qualifications, Mr. Brown, but you haven't worked in marketing.

   B: I know, but _____ .
   advertising

3. A: Let's go to *Gandhi*. We haven't seen it yet.

   B: Yes, but _____ either.
   The Big Chill

4. A: I don't think Harriet is the person for the job. She hasn't worked with large groups.

   B: That's true, but _____ .
   couples and small groups

5. A: Sam Brown can't do the job. He hasn't worked in Spain.

   B: That doesn't matter. _____ .
   Mexico

4. Fill in the blanks to complete the interview. Use present perfect and simple past forms.

A reporter is interviewing Amy Cole about her life.

REPORTER: Ms. Cole, you're a well-known author. How many books _have you written_ ?
1. write

AMY COLE: Well, so far _____ three novels. I _____ *Romance of a*
2. write 3. finish
Lifetime in 1971, *One Autumn in Paris* in 1975 and *Adventure in the Far East* in 1981.

REPORTER: And _____ in many foreign places since you left the United States. How
4. live
many countries have there been?

AMY COLE: At last count, fifteen. I _____ the United States in 1965. That was a long time ago.
5. leave

REPORTER: _____ in China last year, didn't you?
6. travel

AMY COLE: Yes, I _____ two months there.
7. spend

REPORTER: Ms. Cole, _____ a lot of unusual things since you left Boston. Can you
8. do
give me some examples?

AMY COLE: Well, yes. _____ bears in Alaska in 1977. _____ Mount
9. hunt 10. climb
Everest last year. _____ even in jail once!
11. be

REPORTER: In jail? What _____ ?
12. do

AMY COLE: Oh, that's a long story. I think I'll write about it in my next book.

33

I **used to** smoke, but I don't **anymore**.

Didn't you **use to** be a baseball player?
Yes, I **used to** be, but I'm not **anymore**.

1. **Complete the sentences with *used to* and *anymore*.**

1. A: This town has really changed since I was a child.

   B: Yes. *It used to be very peaceful, but it isn't anymore.*
   very peaceful

2. A: Sharon really looks different these days.

   B: Yes. _____
   quite heavy

3. A: The Murrey children have grown up a lot since I saw them last year.

   B: Yes. _____
   really rude

4. A: Bill isn't the way I remember him in college.

   B: No. _____
   get angry a lot

5. A: The kids aren't the way I remember them from my last visit.

   B: No. _____
   be very silly

2. **Complete the statements with *there used to/didn't use to be* or *there is (there's)* or *there are*.**

Past   Present   Past   Present

1. *There used to be* _____ factories by the

   river, but not anymore. Now _____

   a city park.

3. _____ about 50,000

   people in Pleasantville. Now _____

   about 78,000 people.

2. _____ a

   college in Pleasantville, but _____

   one now.

4. _____

   any large department stores downtown. Now

   _____ two—Macy's and Penney's.

| Did you spend any money today? | **A little.** |
| Did you buy any presents? | **A few.** |

Note:

Use **a few** with countable things and **a little** with uncountable things.

1. **The employees of Dexitron Company had an office party. Now it's time to go home. Write *a few* or *a little* in the blanks.**

1. There's ___*a little*___ punch in the bowl.

2. There are just _____ clean glasses left.

3. There are _____ sandwiches left on the tray.

4. There's _____ food left on the table.

5. There's _____ wine left in one bottle.

6. There are _____ potato chips left in the bag.

7. There are just _____ people still at the party.

8. There's just _____ time left until everyone has to leave.

2. **Match the sentences to make conversations. Fill in the blanks with *a few* or *a little*.**

1. How about some more coffee with your dessert, Carlotta?

2. Did you see many plays when you were in New York last summer?

3. I'm going to make some spaghetti. Do we have any tomato sauce?

4. Have you made many friends since you moved to San Francisco?

5. Do you have time to help me with my algebra homework now?

6. How much money do you have with you?

a. Yes, _____. But we're out of spaghetti, and there's no garlic.

b. Just _____. I've been very busy so far, so it's hard to meet people.

c. Well, maybe ___*a little*___. I've already had two large cups.

d. No, just _____. They're very expensive, and I didn't have much money.

e. Just _____. Not enough to buy all those toys.

f. Yes, I have _____ minutes.

MUCH, MANY, A LOT OF

> **How much** (money) can you lend me?
> About 30 dollars.
>
> **How many** (people) have you invited?
> Over 40.
>
> There are going to be **a lot of** people here tonight.
> I have **a lot of** time, but I don't have **a lot of** money.
> She has **a lot of** acquaintances, but not **many** friends.

Note:

A lot of can replace **much** or **many**.

1. Write questions in response to the statements given. Use *how much* or *how many*.

1. A: Mr. Ellis, I need more time to do that!

   B: _How much do you need_ ?

2. A: My sister speaks quite a few languages.

   B: _____ ?

3. A: Sam, I need some people to help me.

   B: _____ ?

4. A: Sarah borrowed some money from me.

   B: _____ ?

5. A: That car really costs a lot.

   B: _____ ?

6. A: Mira has a lot of brothers.

   B: _____ ?

2. Write the questions. Use *much* or *many*.

Lester is asking José about his new life in a small town.

LESTER: Do you make _much_ money in your new job?
          1

JOSE: Not a lot, but that doesn't matter. It's cheaper here.

LESTER: Do you have _____ free time to do the things
                      2
you want to?

JOSE: Yes. That's one of the best things about my job.

LESTER: Have you made _____ new friends?
                        3

JOSE: Yes. And that never happened in the city. We know lots of people here.

LESTER: Is there _____ to do in Bolinas?
                  4

JOSE: Oh, yes. Lots of outdoor activities. Lester, why are you asking me all this? Do you want to move here?

LESTER: I'm thinking about it.

3. **Write negative sentences with *much* or *many*.**

1. A: Why is Claire always so sad?

   B: *She doesn't have many friends.*
   she/have/friends

2. A: Why are you so nervous?

   B: _____
   I/have/time to finish this

3. A: Why did you leave the dance so early?

   B: _____
   I/see/people I know

4. A: Why won't you come to the party with us?

   B: _____
   we/have/fun at big parties.

5. A: Why doesn't she like her home town?

   B: _____
   there/be/excitement there

6. A: Why doesn't Kathy like her new neighborhood?

   B: _____
   there/be/children nearby

7. A: Have a piece of fruit.

   _____
   there/be/calories in an apple

   B: Thanks.

4. **Put these sentences in order and write the conversation.**

1. Have you? They really aren't that difficult. You just need a lot of time to concentrate.
2. I know. I've been having a lot of trouble doing the exercises.
3. Yeah, me too. Well, good luck. See you tomorrow.
4. Time to concentrate? But I have too much to do already.
5. We sure have a lot of homework.

A: *We sure have a lot of homework.*

B: _____

A: _____

_____

B: _____

A: _____

Unit Twenty-Five

All (of) the Olympic athletes are amateurs.	100%
Most (of them) have trained for a very long time.	↕
Some (of them) are men and some are women.	50%
A few (of them) will win gold medals.	↕
None (of them) are professionals.	0%

1. **Fill in the blanks. Use expressions from the grammar box.**

1. _Most of_ the employees are men.

2. _____ them are United States citizens, and _____ them are not.

3. _____ the employees are over 25 years of age. _____ them are over 55 years of age.

4. _____ the employees make over $20,000 a year. _____ them make over $40,000 a year.

EuroBank Employees

Employee	Age	U.S. Citizen	Yearly Salary
Don Battles	35	yes	$26,000
Bill Belkin	38	yes	21,000
Sandra Browne	41	no	34,000
Mary Cook	27	yes	18,000
Martin DeLeon	36	no	39,000
Peter Gomez	48	no	46,000
Jim Jackson	51	yes	38,000
Greg Martin	30	yes	22,000
Otto Muller	43	no	41,000
Bob Rizzuto	36	yes	29,000
Paul Taylor	45	no	45,000

2. **Match the sentences to make conversations. Use expressions from the grammar box to fill in the blanks.**

1. Have you made many friends in Calgary?

2. Mom, can I have some cookies?

3. How much of that job did you get done?

4. Mr. Lee, how many of us failed the quiz?

5. Are all these people coming tonight?

6. Sam, did you finish your math problems?

a. _____ it. I'm ready to do the next job.

b. You can have _____. But don't forget, dinner is in an hour.

c. _A few_, but I haven't been here long. I like the city, though.

d. _____ are, but there are one or two people who can't make it.

e. I did _____ them, but I didn't know how to do about half of them.

f. _____ you. Everyone passed it.

3. Here are the facts about Mr. Bolton's history quiz. Use these facts and expressions from the grammar box to complete his sentences.

> Number of students: 15
>
> Passing grade = 60%
>
> Between 60 and 70%:   3 students
>
> Between 70 and 100%:   12 students
>
> Number of students who missed the question about the Civil War: 7

_____*All of*_____ you _____*passed*_____ the test. _____ you
<u> 1</u>   <u>2. pass</u>   <u> 3</u>

_____ between 60 and 70% of the answers right, but _____ you
<u>4. get</u>   <u> 5</u>

_____ 70% or more. The question about the Civil War was difficult.
<u>6. get</u>

_____ you _____ it, and _____ you didn't.
<u> 7</u>   <u>8. miss</u>   <u> 9</u>

4. Complete the dialogs. Choose from the expressions given.

Some or a few

1. BILL: Did you make any mistakes on the test?

   NANCY: Yeah, _____*Some*_____. My score was 72%. How about you?

   BILL: I made _____ in the first part, but I got 88%.

Some (of) or none (of)

2. HAL: Have you gotten to know many nice men since you moved to Ontario?

   MARY: Yes, a lot. But _____ them are from work. I don't like to socialize with

   the people I work with. _____ them are from a club I joined, and

   _____ are guys who live in the neighborhood.

Most (of) or all (of)

3. STAN: What are the people in your company like?

   PEGGY: _____ them are really nice, but there are a few I don't like.

   _____ them are well educated; everyone has a college degree.

   _____ them are New Yorkers. There are just a few who aren't from

   around here.

The Sears Tower is tall**er than** the Empire State Building.
Los Angeles is big**ger than** San Francisco.
The Amazon is wid**er than** the Mississippi.
Small towns are usually friendl**ier than** big cities.

Note:

Add **-er** to one-syllable words. Add **-r** if the word ends in **e**. For two-syllable words ending in **y**, change the **y** to **i** and add **-er**. Double a final single consonant if it follows a short vowel.

1. **Write the comparative forms of the following adjectives.**

wide _*wider*_   tall _____   nice _____

big _____   thin _____   cheap _____

narrow _____   silly _____   happy _____

2. **Write the comparative form of the words given. Use *than* where necessary.**

Fast Food Craze Hits The United States

Frozen pizzas, T. V. Dinners, Big Macs, french fries, food to go. The fast food industry is growing _*bigger*_ (1. big) every day. Fast food often seems _____ (2. taste) _____ home-made food. It is certainly _____ (3. easy) to prepare. Some people argue that fast food is also _____ (4. cheap). But Roland Wagnalls, author of many books on nutrition says, "People who take the time to eat well-balanced meals are much _____ (5. healthy) and _____ (6. happy). There is no doubt. Fast foods are _____ (7. sweet), _____ (8. salty) and generally more harmful to your health."

So why do people eat junk food? For example, since my friend Sarah started to eat cookies and potato chips at the office, her friends have noticed the change. They all agree that she looked _____ (9. pretty) when she was _____ (10. thin). Sarah complains that her clothes have gotten _____ (11. tight). But she won't admit that she has gained weight. Even worse, she is _____ (12. slow) in everything she does and always seems to feel tired. Sarah is also a good candidate for many illnesses. Statistics show that overweight people are normally _____ (13. sick) the average person.

—JOHN HENDRIX
President, Dairy Association of America

3. Make a comparative statement about each pair of items.

Sahara Desert   **Mojave Desert**

1. *The Sahara Desert is bigger*
   than the Mojave Desert.
   big

Pete   **Jojo**

2. _____
   heavy
   _____

Marianne   **Sue**

3. _____
   tall
   _____

Mt. Everest   **Mt. Kilimanjaro**

4. _____
   high
   _____

4. Fill in the blanks with *which is* or *which are* and comparative forms.

NANCY: *Which is cheaper* _____, life in a big city or in a small town?
       1. cheap

DAD: It's much _____ to live in a small town _____ in a city.
                 2. cheap

NANCY: _____?
       3. safe

DAD: It's _____ in small towns too.
            4. safe

NANCY: _____, cities or small towns?
       5. friendly

DAD: In my experience, people are usually _____ in small towns _____ in cities.
                                            6. friendly

NANCY: _____, cities or small towns?
       7. clean

DAD: Towns are usually _____.
                         8. clean

NANCY: But they're _____, aren't they?
                   9. dull

DAD: Well, small towns are _____, I guess. But you don't have to worry as much.
                            10. dull

NANCY: Hmm. Maybe life is _____ in a small town, but I like cities better.
                          11. easy

DAD: So does your mother.

IRREGULAR COMPARATIVES—*Better, Worse, Farther, Less, More*

This is a **good** book, but that is a **better** one.
Lying is **bad**, but stealing is **worse**.
Mars is **far** from the earth, but Saturn is even **farther**.
Phil ate **a little**, but Bob ate **less**.
Sam eats **a lot**, and Jerry eats even **more**.

1. Write *more, less, farther, better* or *worse* in the blanks.

This year our vacation was ___*better*___ than it was last year. We had much
        ₁
_____ fun this time. Last year we went to Los Angeles and San Diego, but this year
   ₂
we just went to San Francisco. San Francisco is _____ away than Los Angeles, so it
                                    ₃
took an extra day to get there. We had a very restful time once we got there. I think it's
_____ to go to just one place and stay there. There's just one thing that was
   ₄
_____ this year: we had _____ money, so we couldn't buy as much.
   ₅   ₆

2. Complete the questions. Use *better, worse, farther, less* or *more*.

1. A: ___*Which is farther*___ from London, Paris or Berlin?

   B: Berlin is.

2. A: _____ costs _____, a bicycle or a motorcycle?

   B: Are you kidding? A bicycle!

3. A: _____ costs _____, a house or a mobile home?

   B: What a question! A house, of course.

4. A: _____ from the Sun, Jupiter or Saturn?

   B: Saturn is.

5. A: _____ crime do you think _____, robbery or murder?

   B: Murder, I think.

6. A: _____, to be rich or to be famous?

   B: That's a matter of opinion.

7. A: _____, mint chocolate or strawberry?

   B: Well, I like strawberry myself.

REGULAR ADJECTIVE COMPARATIVES—*More + Adjective*

> Miami is **more interesting than** Key West.
> It's also **more crowded**.

Note:

Use **more** to compare adjectives of two or more syllables (except those ending in **y**).

1. **Fill in the blanks. Use *more* plus an adjective comparative form.**

From 1960 to 1980, I lived in Atlanta. In 1980 I moved to Tallahassee, and I like it better here.

Atlanta is _*more interesting than*_ Tallahassee in some ways. Of course, it's
        1. interesting

_____, and it's also _____ Tallahassee.
    2. important   3. exciting

But Atlanta is also _____ and _____. Things
                    4. crowded   5. dangerous

are _____ in Atlanta too. Tallahassee is _____.
        6. expensive   7. peaceful

In my opinion, people in Tallahassee are _____ and
                                             8. polite

_____ people in Atlanta. In general, living in Tallahassee is
        9. respectful

_____ living in Atlanta.
      10. satisfying

2. **Fill in the blanks with *which* and/or comparative forms and correct verbs.**

Alan is asking Jane about her new job as a teacher and her old job as a travel agent.

ALAN: _*Which*_ job _*is more exciting*_?
                         1. exciting

JANE: Well, teaching is. I was bored as a travel agent.

ALAN: _____?
          2. interesting

JANE: Teaching.

ALAN: _____ job _____?
                    3. difficult

JANE: Teaching, definitely!

ALAN: _____ people _____, teachers or travel agents?
                             4. interesting

JANE: They're both interesting.

ALAN: And your new boss? _____ she _____ your old boss?
                                    5. demanding

JANE: No, my boss at the travel agency _____.
                            6. demanding

ALAN: One more question. Is it _____ to be a teacher or a travel agent?
                 7. fun

JANE: For me, being a teacher is more fun.

> For me, math is **the easiest** subject.
> English is **the hardest**.

Note:

Add **-est** to most one-syllable adjectives and some two-syllable adjectives. If a one-syllable adjective ends in **y**, change the **y** to **i** and add **-est**. Double a final single consonant after a short vowel.

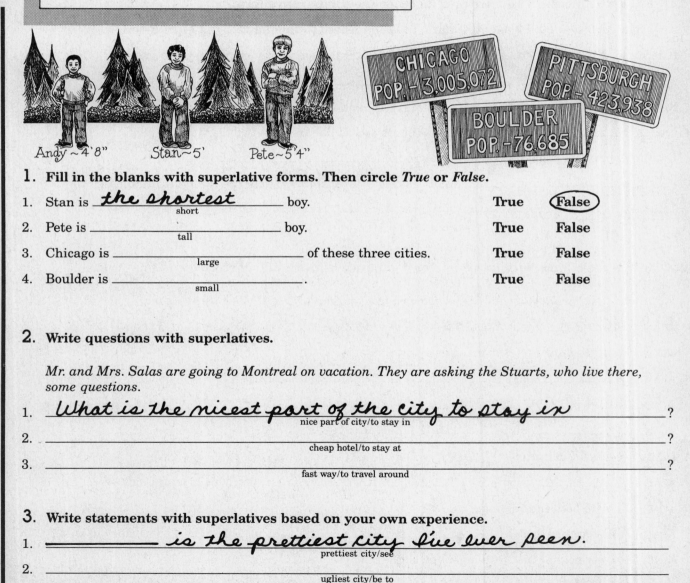

Andy ~ 4'8"   Stan ~ 5'   Pete ~ 5'4"

CHICAGO POP. – 3,005,072
PITTSBURGH POP. – 423,938
BOULDER POP. – 76,685

1. Fill in the blanks with superlative forms. Then circle *True* or *False*.

1. Stan is ___*the shortest*___ boy.   True   (False)
   _{short}

2. Pete is _____ boy.   **True**   **False**
   _{tall}

3. Chicago is _____ of these three cities.   **True**   **False**
   _{large}

4. Boulder is _____.   **True**   **False**
   _{small}

2. Write questions with superlatives.

Mr. and Mrs. Salas are going to Montreal on vacation. They are asking the Stuarts, who live there, some questions.

1. ___*What is the nicest part of the city to stay in*___ ?
   _{nice part of city/to stay in}

2. _____ ?
   _{cheap hotel/to stay at}

3. _____ ?
   _{fast way/to travel around}

3. Write statements with superlatives based on your own experience.

1. _____ *is the prettiest city I've ever seen.*
   _{prettiest city/see}

2. _____
   _{ugliest city/be to}

3. _____
   _{nicest city/be in}

4. _____
   _{oldest city/be in}

REGULAR SUPERLATIVES—*Most and Least*

The Thunderbird is **the most** expensive Ford.
The Escort is **the least** expensive Ford.

Note:

Add **the most** or **the least** to most adjectives of two or more syllables (except those ending in **y**).

1. **Write superlative forms for each of the following adjectives. Use *-est* or *the most*.**

big	*the biggest*	expensive	_____	pretty	_____
important	_____	dangerous	_____	exciting	_____
tall	_____	friendly	_____	rich	_____
old	_____	interesting	_____	intelligent	_____
crowded	_____	cheap	_____	beautiful	_____

2. **Make statements with superlatives. Look at the charts.**

POPULATION DENSITY		
Bangladesh	1,572	
India	513	people per
Nigeria	223	square mile
South Korea	985	

MOTOR VEHICLE DEATH RATES IN 1977		
Costa Rica	21.3	
Japan	10.6	deaths per
Kuwait	36.0	100,000 people
Venezuela	34.2	

1. Bangladesh is *the most crowded* .
   _{crowded}
2. Nigeria is _____ of the four.
   _{crowded}
3. In 1977, Kuwait was _____ of
   _{dangerous}
   these four countries to drive in.
4. Japan was _____ to drive in.
   _{dangerous}

3. **Write sentences based on your own opinion about your country. Use superlatives.**

1. *I think* _____ *is the most beautiful city in*
   _{most beautiful city}
2. _____
   _{least beautiful city}
3. _____
   _{most important city}
4. _____
   _{most interesting place}
5. _____
   _{most exciting place}
6. _____
   _{most dangerous sport}
7. _____
   _{most expensive entertainment}

IRREGULAR SUPERLATIVES

> Anita is **the best** student in the class.
> Jack is **the worst**.
> Anita studies **the most**.
> Jack studies **the least**.
> He also sits **the farthest** from the teacher.

1. Fill in the blanks with *the most, the least, the best, the worst* or *the farthest.*

TEST SCORES		1980 WINTER OLYMPICS		1982 SALARIES ACCOUNTING DEPT.		DISTANCES FROM MEXICO CITY (Km)	
Joe Barstow	**B**	East Germany	23 medals	Adams, John	21,000	Acapulco	400 km
Alice Clark	**B+**	U.S.S.R.	22 medals	Franks, Peter	15,000	Guadalajara	589 km
Ken Foster	**A**	U.S.A.	12 medals	Murrey, Bill	17,000	Mérida	1520 km
Marsha Hammond	**D−**	Norway	10 medals	Nelson, Tom	22,000	Monterrey	952 km
Fred Kraft	**D**	Finland	9 medals			Pueblo	136 km
Stacy Taylor	**F**	Austria	7 medals			Tijuana	2900 km

1. Ken's grade is *the best* .

2. Stacy's grade is _____ .

3. In the 1980 Winter Olympics, East Germany won _____ medals.

4. In 1982, Mr. Franks earned _____ money.

5. Of these six cities, Tijuana is _____ from Mexico City.

2. Jim Jensen is talking to his professor about medical school. Fill in the blanks with *the worst, the best, the most, the least* or *the farthest.*

JIM: Dr. Garvey, I'm considering the University of Houston, the University of Texas, and Johns Hopkins University. Which of these do you think is *the best* ?
    1

DR. GARVEY: It depends. What are you going to specialize in?

JIM: I want to be a surgeon.

DR. GARVEY: Well, Johns Hopkins is _____ for neurosurgery. Houston is
    2

_____ for heart surgery.
    3

JIM: What about tuition?

DR. GARVEY: Well, Johns Hopkins costs _____ . It's very expensive. It's
    4

_____ away from home too. Houston costs _____ of
    5   6

the three. Why don't you stay here in Houston?

JIM: I don't like Houston. It has _____ weather.
    7

COMPARISONS—As + Adjective + As

> John is **as tall as** his brother.
> He's almost **as heavy as** his father.
> San Francisco isn't nearly **as big as** Los Angeles.
> San Diego is about **as big as** San Francisco.

1. **Wendy recently transferred to the University of Kansas. She is telling her friend about it. Complete the dialog with adjectives from the list. Use** *as . . . as.*

friendly   good   happy   expensive   big   hard

KATHY: What do you think of U.K.? Are you happy there?

WENDY: Well, I'm not _as happy as_ I was at Indiana, but it has its good points. Kansas is a

better school for what I want. Indiana's chemistry program isn't _____ the one
2

at Kansas. And Kansas isn't _____ Indiana. Believe it or not, it's
3

three hundred dollars a year cheaper.

KATHY: Is U.K. bigger than Indiana U.?

WENDY: Bigger? No, Kansas isn't nearly _____ Indiana.
4

KATHY: Are the teachers harder here?

WENDY: I don't think they're harder. I guess they're just _____ the teachers at Indiana.
5

The only really bad thing about U.K. is that the people don't seem _____
6

they were at Indiana U. But maybe that's just my first impression.

2. **Complete the dialogs with an adjective from the list. Use** *as . . . as* **or** *not as . . . as.*

smart   important   good   tall

1. A: What do you think of *Superman II*?

   B: Well, it's _not as good as_ *Superman I*, but it's pretty good.

2. A: Did you notice how much Jimmy has grown?

   B: Yes, he isn't a boy anymore. He's _____ his father.

3. A: Which job do you want me to do first?

   B: Anything but the floors. They're _____ the other things.

4. A: Mr. Brown, why is Ben doing poorly in math?

   B: He's not studying, but he can do better. He's just _____ his sisters were.

THE SAME + noun + AS

> I'm **the same size as** my mother.
> Minneapolis is about **the same distance** from LaCrosse **as** Milwaukee.
> My son and my daughter are **the same height as** I am.
> I earn **the same amount** of money **as** my father.

1. **Complete the second line in each conversation. Use the words given.**

   age   size   height   distance   amount

   1. A: Which is bigger, New York or London?

      B: Neither one, really. They're both about _the same size_.

   2. A: Who's older, Jane or Claudia?

      B: _____. They were born in 1953.

   3. A: Who makes more, Ms. Bailey or Ms. Andrews?

      B: _____—$25,000, I think.

   4. A: Who's taller, Jan or Karen?

      B: _____. They can wear the same clothes.

   5. A: Which is farther from Columbus, Cincinnati or Akron?

      B: _____. It takes about two hours to drive to either one.

2. **Complete the sentences. Use *the same . . . as* or comparative forms. Look at the charts.**

   1. Andy is _the same height as_ Bill. They're both
      taller than Jack.
      _{tall}

   2. The Amazon is about _____ the Nile.
      They're both _____ the
      _{long}
      Mississippi.

   3. Osaka is about _____ Yokohama.
      They're both _____ Tokyo.
      _{small}

   4. Jack Green earns about _____
      _____ of money each month _____ Tim
      Jackson. They both earn _____ Joe
      _{little}
      Alcazar.

HEIGHT		
Jack	Andy	Bill
5'8"	5'10"	5'10"

LENGTH		
The Amazon	The Nile	The Mississippi
4,000 miles	4,145 miles	2,348 miles

SIZE		
Osaka	Yokohama	Tokyo
2.6 million	2.7 million	8.2 million

AMOUNT		
Jack Green	Joe Alcazar	Tim Jackson
$1,400 per month	$1,700 per month	$1,425 per month

AS MUCH + AS, AS MANY + AS

> I don't have **as many problems as** I used to.
> My brother earns **as much money as** I do, and he's ten years younger.
> John doesn't eat **as much as** he did before, but he still eats a lot.

1. **Look at the pictures. Complete the sentences with affirmative or negative statements with** *as much as* **or** *as many as.*

1. Alice doesn't have ___*as much money*___ in the bank ___*as*___ Jane.

2. Mr. Brown _____ make _____ each month _____ Mrs. Brown does.

3. The Johnsons _____ have _____ the Riveras do.

4. This semester, Frank _____ teaching _____ Julie is.

5. Cincinnati _____ have _____ San Diego does.

2. **Complete the dialogs with** *as much (as)* **or** *as many (as).* **Use the nouns given.**

> fun   trouble   problems   cigarettes   money   friends

JANET: So, how do you like Miami?

BETTY: We really like it. We don't have ___*as many friends*___ yet as we did in
                                        1
Albuquerque, but that's OK. We don't have _____ either.
                                            2

JANET: Problems? You mean you and Sam?

BETTY: Yeah, you know Sam didn't make _____ I did and that
                                        3
was always a problem. He really likes his new job, and he doesn't have to work such long hours.
The kids love it too. They can have _____ here as they did before.
                                     4
Billy is in a special school, and he doesn't get into _____
                                                      5
he did in Albuquerque.

JANET: What else?

BETTY: Well, people seem much healthier here. They get more exercise for one thing. That has affected all
of us. Sam doesn't smoke _____ he used to.
                          6

NOUN COMPARISONS—More, Less, Fewer + Than

> I make **less** money **than** my brother Stan.
> I have **fewer** problems and **fewer** worries.
> Stan has **more** money and **more** problems.

1. Write questions to fit the answers. Use *more, less* or *fewer*.

1. A: Which city gets _*less*_ rain, Phoenix or Houston?

   B: Phoenix. It got five inches last year. Houston got forty-seven inches.

2. A: Which continent has _____ countries, North America or South America?

   B: North America. There are only three.

3. A: Which country produces _____ oil, Egypt or Saudi Arabia?

   B: Saudi Arabia. It's the second largest oil producer in the world.

4. A: Which city gets _____ snow, Minneapolis or Seattle?

   B: Minneapolis. Seattle doesn't get much snow.

2. Unscramble the sentences.

1. to used I I problems fewer than have.

   I have fewer problems than I used to.

2. I money does son my earn less than.

   _____

3. subjects taking semester last I'm this than fewer.

   _____

4. to used has Bill than friends he more.

   _____

3. Disagree with the statements. Use *less* or *fewer*.

1. A: I don't like San Diego. There's so much crime here.

   B: _Well, there's less than there used to be._

2. A: I don't like this school. There are so many discipline problems.

   B: _____

3. A: I don't like to drive. There are so many accidents these days.

   B: _____

4. A: Let's not drive on Maple Street. There's so much traffic there.

   B: _____

SUPERLATIVES WITH NOUNS—*The Most, The Fewest, The Least*

> Of my brothers, Kevin makes **the most** money and Dan makes **the least**.
> Kevin also has **the most** problems and Dan has **the fewest**.

1. Write sentences using the information in the chart. Use the superlative.

COMPARATIVE SURVEY OF THE FOUR LARGEST COUNTRIES			
	CHINA	INDIA	SOVIET UNION	UNITED STATES
Density	278 people per square mile	519 people per square mile	31 people per square mile	64 people per square mile
Area	3,691,000 square miles	1,269,339 square miles	8,649,490 square miles	3,615,123 square miles
Reserves of Mercury	4.5	—	18.2	8.6
Trade with U.S.	$3,603,000	$1,748,000	$2,431,000	—

1. _India has the most people per square mile_____.
   India/people

2. _____.
   The Soviet Union/people

3. _____.
   The Soviet Union/land

4. _____.
   India/land

5. _____.
   India/reserves of mercury

6. _____.
   China/reserves of mercury

7. _____.
   China/trade

8. _____.
   India/trade

2. Fill in the blanks with *the least, the fewest* or *the most*.

1. A: How was your exam?

   B: Great, I got an *A*. My teacher said I made **the fewest** mistakes of anyone in the class.

2. A: Hi Jim. Did you get the job?

   B: No, and I'm really angry. The guy who got it has _____ experience of all the applicants.

3. A: Look at those beautiful cakes.

   B: I want the one with _____ calories. I'm on a diet.

4. A: What a meal that was! I couldn't tell who ate _____—you, your wife or that man across from you.

   B: I think my wife ate more than anyone at the whole table!

51

ADVERB COMPARISONS

> Who do you think will win the marathon?
> Men usually run **the fastest**.
> Most men run **faster than** women in both the long and short races.
> But some women can run **as fast as** the best men.
>
> Let's go with Harold. He drives **more carefully than** the others.
> Yeah, but not **as carefully as** you do. Let's take our car.
>
> Jack speaks **the most convincingly** of all the candidates.

1. **Make comparative and superlative statements. Look at the chart.**

LIFE SPAN IN CAPTIVITY

LION   30 years

CAT   23 years

PIG   10 years

1. In captivity, lions live _the longest_.
_{long}
Cats live _____ pigs, but they
_{long}
don't live _____ lions.
_{long}

POPULARITY OF DOGS

POODLE   1

DACHSHUND   9

MALTESE   31

2. According to the American Kennel Club,
poodles rank _____
_{high}
in popularity. Dachshunds rank
_____ in the survey, but not
_{low}
_____ Malteses.
_{low}

2. **Unscramble the sentences.**

1. Bob than quickly more works Jerry.   Jerry _works more quickly than Bob._

2. too he intelligently speaks more.   He _____

3. the she responded enthusiastically most.   She _____

4. never more stupidly I've acted.   I've _____

5. I you well Portuguese as speak as do.   You _____

REQUESTS and SUGGESTIONS

What **should we do** tonight? **Let's go** to a movie. No, **why don't we** go to that concert?	**Let's not** invite the Smiths again, OK? Why not? They're always fighting.

1. **Fill in the blanks. Use** *let's*, *let's not*, *should* **or** *why don't we*.

JEAN: Alan, what _Should we do_ tonight? _____ dinner, or do you want to
1. we/do   2. I/make

go out?

ALAN: No, don't make dinner. _____ . _____ to that new
3. go out   4. go

Indian restaurant?

JEAN: No, _____ there. I don't feel like Indian food. _____ to that
5. go   6. go

Chinese restaurant on Garden Street.

2. **Match the sentences to make conversations. Fill in the blanks with** *should*, *let's* **or** *let's not*.

1. _Let's_ go to the movies.

2. _____ go to that concert?

3. What _____ do today?

4. _____ open the window?

5. _____ ask the Adamses for
dinner too?

6. _____ get Davy a dog for
Christmas?

a. _____ stay home and rest.

b. No, _let's not_ . We went to the movies
last night.

c. No, _____ invite them. They're
always fighting.

d. OK, _____ . I love Mozart.

e. Great idea. He loves animals.

f. No, I'm too cold aready.

3. **Fill in the blanks with** *why don't we*, *let's* **or** *let's not*.

STEVE: The real estate agent called again. She said the house we like wasn't sold over the weekend.
Should we buy it?

JESSICA: _Let's not_ be too eager. _____ think about it until tomorrow.
1   2

STEVE: But, _____ wait too long or someone else may buy it.
3

JESSICA: _____ tell the agent that we're very interested, but it's too much money?
4

STEVE: Oh, I don't know. _____ forget the whole thing.
5

JESSICA: Come on. _____ get upset. _____ go to sleep and get
6   7

some rest?

WOULD LIKE, WOULD RATHER, HOW ABOUT

What **would** you **like** to do tonight?
Would you **like** to go to a movie?
Not really, **I'd rather** do something else.
Like what?
Well, **how about** going dancing?
Yeah, **I'd like** that.

What **would** you **like** to do for your birthday?
I'd rather not celebrate it this year.
Oh, come on. You're not that old!

1. **The Salazars are moving to the United States. Fill in the blanks with** *would like* **or** *would rather* **plus a verb. Then look at Juan's chart and answer** *True* **or** *False*.

Dad wants	Mom wants	Maria and I want
to live in a big city	to live in the suburbs	to live in a small town
to rent an apartment	to buy a house	to buy a house
to have a dog	to have a cat	to have a horse
to buy a Chevrolet	to buy a Toyota	to buy a Ford

1. Mr. Salazar _would like to live_ in a big city. (**True**) False

2. Mrs. Salazar _would rather live_ in the suburbs. **True** False

3. Juan and María _____ in a small town. **True** False

4. Mr. Salazar _____ an apartment. **True** False

5. Mrs. Salazar and the children _____ a house. **True** False

6. Mr. Salazar _____ a cat. **True** False

7. Mrs. Salazar _____ a dog. **True** False

8. Juan and María _____ a horse. **True** False

9. Mr. Salazar _____ a Chevrolet. **True** False

10. Mrs. Salazar _____ a Toyota. **True** False

11. The children _____ a Ford. **True** False

2. Complete the dialog. Use a form of *would like ('d like)*, *would rather ('d rather)* or *how about.*

STEVE: Alice, where _would you like_ to go on our vacation this year?

ALICE: I'm not sure. I think _I'd like_ to go out west again.
                              (2)

STEVE: Sounds good to me.

ALICE: _____(3)_____ go to the Coast or to Arizona and Colorado—that area?

STEVE: I think _____(4)_____ go to California.

ALICE: OK. Where in California? Los Angeles or San Francisco?

STEVE: _____(5)_____ go to Los Angeles. They say it's too hot.

ALICE: Oh, it's not that hot. _____(6)_____ taking the kids to Disneyland and Universal Studios?

STEVE: _____(7)_____ that, wouldn't they? Bobby always says he's the only one in his class who hasn't been to Disneyland.

ALICE: So, _____(8)_____ spending a week in each place?

STEVE: OK. But let's see what the kids think.

3. Fill in the blanks with *would like ('d like)* or *would rather ('d rather)*. Then answer these questions about yourself.

1. _Would you rather_ be good looking or intelligent?

   I'd rather be _____ .

2. _____ to spend a week in Moscow? Or _____

   _____ go to London?

   _____ .

3. _____ live in a big city or a small town?

   _____ .

4. What _____ eat, hamburgers or tacos?

   _____ .

5. What _____ to do tonight?

   _____ .

> I'll be home late tonight.
> I **won't** be here in time for dinner.
>
> **Will** we solve the problem of overpopulation in the next 50 years?
> I hope we **will**.

Note:

Use **will** with nouns, and with pronouns joined by *and*.
Jerry and I will go home tomorrow.

Use **will** with short answers.
Yes, we will.

Usually use **'ll** with *I, you, he, she, we* and *they*.
They'll see you tomorrow.

1. **John Dawson is talking to his mother on the telephone. Fill in the blanks with *will*, *'ll* or *won't* plus a verb.**

JOHN: Hi, Mom. I'm coming to Minneapolis on business. I <u>'ll be</u> there next Tuesday night.
1. be

MOM: Oh, John, that's wonderful news. Your father _____ so pleased.
2. be

JOHN: Oh, _____ back by then?
3. Dad/be

MOM: Yes, he's coming home tomorrow night.

JOHN: I'm glad.

MOM: John, _____ here in time for dinner?
4. get

JOHN: The plane gets in at about 10:00 so I _____ it for dinner. But
5. make

I_____ the night, and we can have breakfast together.
6. spend

MOM: What time should we meet you?

JOHN: Don't worry about it. I_____ a taxi at the airport, and I_____ you at home
7. get 8. see

about 10:30.

2. **Dr. Smithson, director of the Brookline Research Institute, is talking about life in the twenty-first century. Ask him questions with** *will*.

1. A: _Will we have another world war_ ?
      have another world war
   B: I'm not sure, but I don't think so.

2. A: _____?
      run out of oil
   B: Yes, probably. Oil is already scarce.

3. A: _____?
      use nuclear power
   B: It's doubtful. Many people think it's too dangerous.

4. A: _____?
      travel to other planets
   B: I think we will. We'll have to find more space to live in.

5. A: _____?
      a lot of people have test tube babies
   B: Maybe not a lot, but more than at present.

6. A: _____?
      people still eat meat
   B: Yes, but less than they do now.

Now write three questions you would like to ask him.

7. _____?

8. _____?

9. _____?

3. **Complete the conversations. Use** *'ll* **and** *be here* **or** *be there*.

1. A: Are you going to the party?
   B: Yes. _I'll be there_ by 8:00.

2. A: Is John coming home for dinner?
   B: Yes. _____ at 6:30.

3. A: Are you transferring to U.C.L.A.?
   B: Yes. _____ for two years.

4. A: Is Jim going to Camp Pendleton for his military service?
   B: Yes. _____ for ten weeks.

5. A: Is Mary coming to class today?
   B: Yes. _____ in a few minutes.

6. A: Has the plane arrived yet?
   B: No, but _____ by 4:30.

WILL—Requests and Offers

> **Will** you lend me some money?
> Of course **I will**. How much do you need?
>
> Mom, my zipper is stuck.
> Come here. I**'ll** fix it for you.
>
> I don't have time to do the dishes tonight.
> **Will** you do them for me?
> No, I **won't**. I did them last night.
> Then I**'ll** do them tomorrow.

1. **Write request questions with** *will.*

1. A: I need someone to type my paper.

   B: I'm a good typist.

   A: ___*Will you type it for me*___ ?
   _{type}

   B: Sure.

2. A: I need someone to fix my car. _____ ?
   _{fix}

   B: No, why should I?

3. A: I need someone to fix that fence. _____ ?
   _{fix}

   B: Yeah, is tomorrow OK?

4. A: I need someone to take care of my car while I'm gone. _____ ?
   _{do}

   B: No, I'm sorry. I really don't want the responsibility.

5. A: I have to pick Jenny up at school, but the car won't start. _____ ?
   _{pick her up}

   B: What time?

2. **Make offers. Use** *'ll* **or** *will.*

1. I need to wash these windows, but I can't reach them.

   Don't worry. ___*I'll wash them for you.*___
   _I

2. I have to do the dishes, but I just don't have the energy right now.

   Don't worry. _____ .
   _I

3. I need to change the oil in my car, but I don't know how.

   That's all right. _____ .
   _{Bob}

4. I have to pick up the children, but I don't have time.

   Oh well. _____ .
   _{Mary and I}

5. I need to type my paper, but my typing is horrible.

   Don't worry. _____ .
   _{Betty}

3. Fill in the blanks in the story. Use *will ('ll)* or *won't* and appropriate verbs.

One day the little red hen found a grain of wheat in the barnyard and decided to plant it.

"Who __*will help*__ me plant the wheat?" she asked the other animals. "Not I," said the
<u>1. help</u>

duck. "I _____," said the pig. "I _____ either," said the dog. "Then I _____
<u>2</u>   <u>3</u>   <u>4</u>

plant it myself," said the little red hen. And she did.

Soon the seed came up and grew into a tall plant. "Who _____ me cut
<u>5. help</u>

the wheat?" asked the little red hen. "I _____," said the pig. "Me neither," said the dog.
<u>6</u>

"I _____," said the duck. "Then I _____ it myself," said the little red hen.
<u>7</u>   <u>8. cut</u>

And she did.

Now the wheat was ready to be made into flour. "Who _____ the wheat to the
<u>9. take</u>

mill?" the little red hen said. "Not I," said the dog. "Nor I," said the pig. "And of course I

_____," said the duck. "Then I _____ it myself," said the little red
<u>10</u>   <u>11. take</u>

hen. And she did.

The mill ground the wheat into a sack of flour. The little red hen brought the flour home and

decided to make some bread. "Who _____ me bake the bread?" asked the
<u>12. help</u>

little red hen. "None of us _____," answered the three animals. "We're too busy." "Then I
<u>13</u>

_____ it myself," the little red hen said. And she did.
<u>14. bake</u>

Soon the bread was ready, and it smelled wonderful. "Who _____ me eat
<u>15. help</u>

the bread?" asked the little red hen. "I _____," said the dog. "I _____ too,"
<u>16</u>   <u>17</u>

said the pig. "Me too," said the duck. "Oh, no you _____," said the little red
<u>18</u>

hen. "You didn't help me plant the wheat, or cut it, and take it to the mill or bake the bread. So

you _____ it. I _____ it myself!" And she did.
<u>19. eat</u>   <u>20. eat</u>

POSSIBILITY—*May, Might, Could*

Are you going to class tomorrow?
I haven't decided yet. I **might** or I **might not**.

Where's Phillip?
He **may be** at the library. He said he had to do a report.

Why are they so late?
I don't know. They **could be** stuck in traffic.

1. Match the sentences to complete the conversations.

1. Is Professor Li going to teach the class?
2. What are your friends doing tonight?
3. Where are the kids now?
4. What can Peter do about his job?
5. Are you and Sam going to fly home soon?
6. There have been lots of floods. This road is dangerous now.
7. When will your son be home from Europe?

a. I don't know. They may be going dancing.
b. I'm not sure. They might be next door.
c. I don't know, but it could be any day.
d. He may. It depends on his schedule.
e. I know. It could cave in.
f. He could talk it over with his boss.
g. We may. We've been thinking about going home for Christmas.

2. Fill in the blanks with *might* or *might not*.

SUSAN: Are you going to take a vacation this year?

MIKE: I'm not sure. I _might_ or I _____.

SUSAN: If you do take one, where will you go?

MIKE: Well, I don't know. I _____ go to Montreal, or I _____ hitchhike to Mexico City.

SUSAN: Which would you rather do?

MIKE: Hitchhike, I think. Actually, I _____ hitchhike all the way. Maybe I'll take the bus from El Paso to Mexico City. If I do that, I _____ ask Dave to come along too.

SUSAN: Why don't you go to Acapulco?

MIKE: Well, I'm low on money. I _____ have enough to get that far.

SUSAN: Can't you get a loan?

MIKE: Yeah, I _____ do that.

CAN'T, COULDN'T, MIGHT NOT as PROBABILITY

> Look. There's Jane.
>
> That **can't**
> **couldn't** be Jane. She's in Florida.

> We **might not** go to Spain after all.
> Why not?
> It's too expensive.

---

1. Complete the sentences with *can't* or *might not*.

1. A: How old is Sue?

   B: Forty-five, I think.

   A: She _**can't**_ be. She looks about 30.

2. A: Jim and I are getting married.

   B: What! You _____ be. You've only known each other a week.

3. A: I _____ be able to come this weekend. I have a lot of work to do. I'll let you know on Tuesday, OK?

   B: Yeah, that's fine. Give me a call.

4. A: Isn't that Katy over there?

   B: It _____ be Katy. She's in Miami.

5. A: Are your friends skiing in Aspen?

   B: They _____ be. There isn't any snow yet.

6. A: Will you graduate this June?

   B: I _____. I won't know for a couple of months.

7. A: Do you think we can get tickets to *La Cage Aux Folles* this Saturday?

   B: You _____. It's hard to get tickets on weekends.

8. A: I think that's the man who stole your wallet.

   B: It _____ be. He was much taller.

2. Complete the headlines. Use *could* or *couldn't*.

The Economy

Bad news. Interest rates _**Could**_₁ go up by the end of the year. 4

Freeze destroys crops. Conditions _____₂ be worse for Midwest farmers. 6

Home Life

Canadian couple wins $11 million in lottery. "We _____₃ be happier." 7

Science

A successful space shuttle _____₄ lead to amazing discoveries in space. 9

Sports

Tigers' final win _____₅ bring them their first pennant since 1962. 11

Cities

Plans to rebuild Newton Library fail. "We _____₆ get enough money without a miracle." 12

MUST as PROBABILITY

> Mrs. Grant lives in a mansion. She **must be** rich.
> Jim isn't answering his telephone. He **must not be** home.
> I hear water running. Someone **must be** taking a bath.

Note:

Must can be followed by a simple verb form or by **be** and a verb with **-ing**.

Must in its probability meaning is not contracted with **not**.

1. **Complete the sentences. Use** *must* **or** *must not* **and other necessary words.**

1. It ___*must be*___ fall.

2. Alice _____ in love.

3. It _____ cold.

4. Frances _____ a good swimmer.

5. Mrs. Joseph _____ feel very well.

2. **Fill in the blanks. Use** *must be* **or** *must not be* **and the words given.**

a smoker   *planning to get married*   *a fire*   *in love*   *on a diet*

1. A: Listen . . . I hear sirens.

   B: Yes. There ___*must be a fire*___.

2. A: Joe hasn't called Sarah in a week.

   B: Yeah, he _____ anymore.

3. A: I saw Randy buying a ring yesterday.

   B: He _____.

4. A: Susan isn't eating much these days.

   B: She _____.

5. A: There are ashtrays all over the house.

   B: Someone here _____.

3. You have been invited to a party. You don't know the people very well, and you've never been to the house before. Make sentences with *must* about what you assume.

1. The house is a mansion and there are two Rolls-Royces in the driveway.

   They _**must be rich**_ .

2. There are pictures of very fat people on the refrigerator.

   Someone _____ .

3. There are many abstract paintings on the walls.

   They _____ modern art.

4. You hear a barking noise.

   They _____ a _____ .

5. Suddenly you smell smoke.

   Something _____ .

4. Unscramble the sentences.

1. ring wearing a she's./ she married be must.

   She's wearing a ring. She must be married.

2. door the answering is no one./ out be must they.

   _____

3. the I can't blackboard see./ glasses must need I new.

   _____

4. number book telephone can't I their the in find./ anymore not they here must live.

   _____

   _____

I'm really angry at Jim.
You **shouldn't** be. It's not his fault.

I want to see her. **Should** I call her?
No, you **should** wait a day or two.

Nancy is always having trouble with her car.
Yes. She **ought to** get a new one.

Note:

Ought to is equivalent to **should**.
Ought to is rare in questions and negatives.

1. Read the letter from Desperate. Then write Pamela's advice. Use *should*.

Dear Pamela,
    I am very unhappy. I've been having a lot of problems lately. My boss makes me so nervous that I've been smoking over two packs of cigarettes a day. Plus, I almost never get any exercise anymore, so I've been feeling bad. I left high school last year. At first I was really glad to get out. Now, my job seems more boring than school. My mother says I should go back to school or move out. Some mom, huh? So what should I do?
                                                                    Desperate

Dear Desperate,

    Here's my advice.

You ___*should quit smoking*_____.
        1. keep smoking/quit smoking

You _____
        2. get more exercise/get less exercise

You _____
        3. go back to school/forget about school

You _____
        4. stay where you are/find your own apartment

                        Good luck,   *Pamela*

2. Complete these letters to Pamela.

Dear Pamela,

I have a terrible problem. My girlfriend is seeing another man. What **should I do** (1)? _____ (2) stop seeing her? _____ (3) tell her I know what she's doing? Or _____ (4) pretend nothing has happened? And what about her? _____ (5) apologize to me?

Broken-Hearted and Puzzled

Dear Broken-Hearted and Puzzled,

_____ (6) pretend that everything is all right, but _____ (7) be cruel to her, either. Tell her exactly how you feel. Say that you want your relationship to continue and that the two of you _____ (8) to be honest with each other. You'll be happier if you express your feelings. Of course, she may choose the other man. But that's always a risk.

Pamela

3. Give advice in the following situations. Use *ought to* or *shouldn't*.

Situation 1: A: Leslie looks so tired.

B: I know. She **ought to** take a vacation.

Situation 2: A: The doctors told me to go on a diet.

B: Then you _____ have any of my dark double chocolate and whipped cream cake. What a shame!

Situation 3: A: Pam is always sleepy in class.

B: She _____ stay up so late at night.

Situation 4: A: I'm not feeling very well.

B: Then you _____ go out tonight.

Situation 5: A: I almost hit that car. Did you see that?

B: Of course I saw that! You really _____ be more careful.

Situation 6: A: You _____ call home more often.

B: I know. But I've been so busy.

> You**'d better** wear your heavy coat. It's going to snow.
>
> It's late. **Hadn't** we **better** leave now?
> Yes. The buses will stop running soon.
>
> We**'d better not** tell Mom.
> Yeah, she'll be furious.

1. **Look at the pictures and fill in the blanks with** *had ('d) better*. **Use the verbs given.**

put out   *stop*   *take*   *start*   *slow down*

1. Mr. Harvey *had better take* an umbrella with him.

2. Mary is in a hurry, but she _____.

3. Her guests will be here in an hour. Sandra _____ dinner.

4. This man _____ his cigarette.

5. The driver _____ at the next gas station.

2. **Fill in the sentences to make conversations. Write in** *'d better not* **or** *'d better*.

1. A: Uh-oh, Bobby, we broke that window.

   B: Listen, we *'d better not* say anything.

2. A: Clifford only gets four hours of sleep a night.

   B: Yeah, but he _____ keep it up. If he does, he'll have a nervous breakdown.

3. A: Look how late it is.

   B: I know. We _____ start studying.

4. A: Oh no, Mom, I broke a plate.

   B: Next time you _____ carry so many things at once.

5. A: I think those pants are too tight on you.

   B: Boy, I _____ go on a diet.

6. A: Where are your friends?

   B: I don't know. They _____ hurry or they'll miss the first part of the show.

─MUST/HAVE TO─

> We **don't have to** go to the party if you don't want to.
> But you **must** call and tell them we won't be there.
> You **mustn't** forget. They would never forgive us.

1. Joe is at the doctor's office. Complete the doctor's statements with *must* or *mustn't*.

DOCTOR: Joe, you already know what I'm going to tell you. You simply ___*must*___ go on a diet.
1

And you _____ start getting more exercise. Why don't you try jogging or
2

swimming?

JOE: But, Doctor, is it safe for me to exercise at my age?

DOCTOR: Of course, but you _____ do too much at first. Also, I'm putting you on a special diet
3

for a few weeks. You _____ eat fatty foods or sweets. Don't drink any alcohol either.
4

JOE: What about beer?

DOCTOR: No, you _____ drink any beer or wine either. And one more thing. You absolutely
5

_____ stop smoking.
6

JOE: You're asking for a lot!

2. Respond to the questions. Use *mustn't* or *don't/doesn't have to*.

1. A: Shall I speak to Mr. Pierce about your problem?

   B: No, no, ___*you mustn't*___ do that! He'll get angry.

2. A: Should James come by in the morning and pick you up?

   B: No, _____ . I'll get a ride later.

3. A: Doctor, what can Bob eat?

   B: Just about everything, but _____ have any chocolate.

4. A: Should I give him his medicine every hour?

   B: No, _____ take it that often. That wouldn't be good for him.

5. A: Can I come over to your house tonight?

   B: No, _____ come! My wife will be furious.

6. A: Do you want me to do the dishes?

   B: No, _____ . I have time to do them.

7. A: Doctor, should I make an appointment for next week?

   B: No, _____ . Next month will be fine.

I **couldn't** swim a year ago, but I **can** now.

Will you be here tomorrow?
No, I **won't**.

What do you think I **should** do?
I think you **ought to** sell your house.

Can I see you tomorrow instead? I **have to** finish this report right now.
Of course. It **must** be very important.

Would you **like** to have a Coke?
Thanks, I**'d rather** have some tea.

What are you doing tonight?
Oh, I **might** stay home or I **may** go out.
Should I give you a call?
Yes. Maybe we **can** get together.

1. **Choose the correct modal to fill in the blanks.**

NURSE: Dr. Gold's office. _Can_ I help you?
        _{1. should/can}

BILL FOX: Yes, this is Bill Fox. _____ I speak to Dr. Gold?
        _{2. can't/can}

NURSE: Dr. Gold is out of town. He _____ be back until Tuesday.
        _{3. won't/mustn't}

BILL FOX: That's terrible. I really _____ speak to him. It's urgent.
        _{4. will/must}

NURSE: Oh, you _____ be the gentleman who called before. What's the problem?
        _{5. must/ought to}

BILL FOX: My little girl is very sick. She _____ breathe very well, and she has a pain in her side.
        _{6. can't/won't}

I think she _____ have appendicitis.
        _{7. will/might}

NURSE: My goodness. That is serious. Let me see. I _____ give you a number in Kansas City.
        _{8. would rather/can}

He _____ be at his hotel; I'm not sure. Or _____ I try to connect you?
        _{9. might/must}   _{10. will/should}

BILL FOX: Please try to connect me. Doctors _____ be in their offices when their patients
        _{11. ought to/would rather}

need them.

NURSE: There's no answer. _____ I keep trying, or _____
        _{12. can/should}   _{13. would you rather/would you like}

call back?

BILL FOX: I _____ call back in 15 minutes. Please keep trying until then.
        _{14. 'll/ought to}

NURSE: Yes, I _____. I think you _____ keep your daughter quiet, and make
        _{15. will/should}   _{16. will/should}

her lie down.

2. **Complete the sentences to make conversations. Fill in the blanks with modals.**

1. A: What are you going to do tomorrow?

   B: I ___*may*___ play tennis if it doesn't rain.
   'd rather/may

2. A: What _____ I get at the store this afternoon?
   may/should

   B: Get some hamburger and some rice for dinner.

3. A: _____ have steak or shrimp tonight?
   would you rather/won't you

   B: I think I _____ have the steak.
   would rather/must

4. A: Who do you think _____ win the election?
   will/must

   B: Senator Grabble, I think.

5. A: Acme Corporation. _____ I help you?
   should/can

   B: Yes, this is Jim Curtis. _____ I speak to Mrs. Malone?
   can/will

6. A: I don't see Mary in class today.

   B: Yeah, she _____ be sick with the flu that's going around.
   must/can't

7. A: _____ you see the game from your seats?
   can/should

   B: We _____ see it, but not very well because we're too far back.
   ought to/can

3. **Complete the conversations with negative forms of modals.**

1. A: Why didn't you like the concert?

   B: I ___*couldn't*___ hear very well. We were in the balcony.
   mustn't/couldn't

2. A: Why don't you want to go swimming?

   B: Because I _____ swim. I never learned.
   can't/'d rather not

3. A: Why don't you want to have steak?

   B: Because I ate it last night, and I _____ eat it again.
   'd rather not/couldn't

4. A: Why can't Joe have Coke?

   B: Because the doctor told him he _____ have anything sweet.
   might not/shouldn't

5. A: Why are you doing your homework now?

   B: I'm going out tonight, and I _____ have time to do it.
   might not/couldn't

6. A: Why did you hide my cigarettes?

   B: Because you _____ smoke so much.
   couldn't/shouldn't

People **are supposed to** obey the speed limit, but they don't always.
People **aren't supposed to** speed, but sometimes they do.

You **weren't supposed to** bring the hamburgers.
What **was** I **supposed to** bring?
Hot dogs.

1. Fill in the blanks with affirmative and negative forms of *be supposed to*.

Dear Sandra,

I've made it through my first week of teaching. I can't believe it. Mr. Jackson, the principal, gave me a very official-looking list of rules. But no one seems to obey them.

Students *are supposed to*₁ be on time to class. If they're late, I

_____₂ report them. Well, someone is always late. They

_____₃ be quiet in class. Some of them are, but there's always at least

one student who doesn't want to study. Students _____₄ do their

homework every night. But some of them have jobs and don't always have time. A student

_____₅ chew gum in class. But sometimes they forget. Students

_____₆ run in the halls, or teachers either. I have to remember that

when I'm late for my first class!

I'll let you know how next week goes. What do you

2. The Palmers and the Millers are planning a picnic. Fill in the blanks with present and past forms of *be supposed to*.

JIM PALMER: OK, *what are we supposed to bring*_{1. we/bring} ?

ALICE MILLER: Hamburgers. The Gomezes are bringing hot dogs.

JOANNE PALMER: ______{2. we/bring} the buns too?

ALICE MILLER: Yes. Now let's see . . . I ______{3. bring} the wine

and Sally ______{4. bring} beer.

Later, at the picnic

JOANNE PALMER: OK, here are the hot dogs.

ALICE MILLER: Oh, no, Joanne! You ______{5. bring} hot dogs.

I told Jim you ______{6. bring} hamburgers.

JOANNE PALMER: Oh, sorry.

INFINITIVE OF PURPOSE

Why did you take the car to the garage? **To get** it fixed.

I came **to talk** to you about the new project.

I am writing **in order to** inquire about job possibilities with your company.

Note:

In order to is more formal than **to**.

1. Recently MODERN TEEN did a survey to find out why students go to college. Here is what they found out. Complete the sentences with infinitives of purpose. Add other words if necessary.

MODERN TEEN

1. 50% say they go to college *to get a good job.*
   get/good job

2. 40% go _____
   find/someone/marry

3. 60% say they go _____
   please/parents

4. 80% say they go _____
   have/good time

5. 30% say they go _____
   get/education

2. Fill in the blanks. Use the words and phrases given.

better their situation   *provide for their families*   *find jobs*   *escape*

make money   *start a new life*   *satisfy*

WHY ARE IMMIGRANTS STILL COMING TO AMERICA?

Professor Mark Mannocchi of Cramdon State University says that many people are still coming to America *to start a new life*₁. One of the main reasons why they still come is _____₂ in order _____₃ better. They feel that America is still the place to get these jobs. Others come _____

_____₄ poor living conditions in their native countries. Many others come with no plans to stay. They just come _____₅ and take it back home. Some people come _____

_____₆ a taste for adventure. All come _____

_____₇ in some way.

> Let's go to Bear Mountain this weekend.
> OK, but I don't know **how to get** there.
> That's all right, I know.
> Are you sure you know **where to get off** the expressway?
> Yes. We take Exit 29.

1. Fill in the blanks. Use the phrases given and *who, where, how* or *what*.

to bring   *to get here*   *to ask*   *to type*   *to send them*

1. A: Is Mary coming to the party?

    B: I'm afraid not. I forgot to tell her *how to get here* _____.

2. A: Is Kathy bringing anything to drink?

    B: I'm not sure. I didn't tell her _____.

3. A: Did Mr. Wilson type those reports?

    B: I doubt it. He doesn't know _____.

4. A: Did she send out those letters?

    B: I don't think so. I didn't tell her _____.

5. A: Are you coming to the dance?

    B: No, I didn't know _____.

2. Complete the conversations with negative statements. Use information question words plus infinitives and pronouns, if necessary.

1. A: Why didn't you do your homework?

    B: *I didn't know how to do it* _____.
        _{how}

2. A: Why didn't you send out those letters?

    B: _____.
        _{where}

3. A: Why didn't Sally buy the tickets?

    B: _____.
        _{how many}

4. A: Why didn't Jim bring my book?

    B: _____.
        _{which one}

5. A: Why didn't you buy a present?

    B: _____.
        _{what}

3. Complete the letters to Pamela. Choose from the phrases given.

who to ask   how to run   where to go   how to manage
how to have   where to get   what to do   how to accept

ADVICE—All your questions answered

Dear Pamela

DEAR PAMELA:
I've really been having a lot of problems lately with my daughter, Martha. She's 25 years old, but she doesn't know ___how to___ ___manage___ her life. She knows _____ fun and _____ a good meal—which is at home, of course. She also knows _____ for money—her father. I've tried to teach her to live life successfully, but apparently I haven't taught her _____ responsibility. Any suggestions? I don't know _____.

—PUZZLED IN KANSAS

DEAR PUZZLED IN KANSAS:
You can't teach a 25-year-old woman _____ _____ her life. That's her job. But you can tell her _____: out of your house. Tell her you think it's time for her to move into her own apartment. She has to learn to be on her own sometime.

4. Choose words from each column and make appropriate questions for these answers.

Can you show me	who	to go
Do you know	what	to turn
Does he know	how long	to do
Do you remember	where	to ask
Do the instructions say	how	to cook the turkey

1. A: ___Do the instructions say what to do___ ?

   B: No, but they say what *not* to do.

2. A: _____ ?

   B: Sure. Push your right ski out from your body like this.

3. A: _____ ?

   B: Yeah. The office is on the third floor.

4. A: _____ ?

   B: Cook it until it's done.

5. A: _____ ?

   B: Yeah, he should ask his teacher.

73

NOUN CLAUSE OBJECTS

Can you tell me **if there's a grocery store around here**?
I don't know **if there's one or not**.

What do you know about Jim?
I know **that he's a successful businessman**.
Is he married?
I don't know **whether he's married or not**.

Note:

In noun clauses introduced by **that**, we often omit **that** in informal speech and writing.
I know **that he's a doctor**. OR I know **he's a doctor**.

1. **When Mrs. Bean came home, there was a burglar in her house. She called the police. Complete her answers with *if* or *that*.**

OFFICER: Was he young or old?

MRS. BEAN: I think that he was (1. be) a younger man—about 20.

OFFICER: Did he take any money? Any jewelry?

MRS. BEAN: I don't know ______ (2. take) money or not. He took a watch and my favorite diamond earrings!

OFFICER: Do you know ______ (3. take) anything else?

MRS. BEAN: I don't know.

OFFICER: Well, what *do* you know?

MRS. BEAN: I know ______ (4. be) in a hurry. He broke a vase.

I know ______ (5. smoke). He left a cigarette burning.

I know ______ (6. wear) tennis shoes. I found a footprint.

OFFICER: All right, Mrs. Bean, we'll send someone over to investigate.

MRS. BEAN: Thank you.

2. **Fill in the blanks. Use *whether* and any other necessary words.**

1. A: Do you know *whether my check came or not* ?
   my check/come

   B: Yes, it came yesterday.

2. A: Do you know _____ ?
   Mary/come/to the party

   B: She said that she's coming.

3. A: Do you know _____ ?
   I/pass/the course

   B: Yes, you passed with a *B*.

4. A: Do you know _____ ?
   I/can use/my credit cards

   B: Yes. They accept all major credit cards.

3. **You are a tourist in a strange city. Complete the questions with *if*.**

1. Can you tell me *if there's a post office near here* ?
   a post office near here

2. Do you know _____ ?
   the buses run all night

3. Can you tell me _____ ?
   a place to wash clothes around here

4. Can you tell me _____ ?
   an inexpensive restaurant in the neighborhood

5. Do you know _____ ?
   a place to cash a check on Saturdays

6. Can you tell me _____ ?
   stores accept traveler's checks

4. **Karl's girlfriend, who rents an apartment from Mrs. Cassaday, has disappeared. Karl is talking to Mrs. Cassaday on the phone. Use *whether* or *that* to complete the dialog.**

KARL: Do you know *whether she left last night* ?
1. leave/last night

MRS. CASSADAY: How should I know?

KARL: Can you tell me _____ ?
2. come back/early this morning

MRS. CASSADAY: No. I don't know _____ or not.
3. come back

KARL: Do you know _____ ?
4. take/any luggage

MRS. CASSADAY: Yes, the doorman said _____ one small suitcase.
5. take

KARL: Do you have any idea where she might be?

MRS. CASSADAY: No, I don't. I'm sorry.

| I know a lot about you. | I know | what your name is.
where you live.
who you're married to.
how old you are.
when you moved to this city.
why you're here.
whose fault it is. |

1. **Mr. Wong has been in an accident and can't remember anything. Use the conversation to complete Officer O'Reilly's report.**

O'REILLY: What's your name?

WONG: I don't know.

O'REILLY: Where do you live?

WONG: I can't remember.

O'REILLY: What time did the accident happen?

WONG: I don't know.

O'REILLY: How old are you?

WONG: I'm not sure.

O'REILLY: Who was driving the other car?

WONG: I didn't see.

O'REILLY: What do you do for a living?

WONG: I can't remember.

O'REILLY: Whose fault was the accident?

WONG: I don't know.

Mr. Cheng Ho Wong
173 So. Orange Avenue
So. Orange, NJ 07079

Mr. Wong doesn't know *what his name is*   .
                                      1. name

He can't remember _____ .
                                        2. live

_____ .
                                        3. accident

_____ .
                                        4. old

_____ .
                                        5. car

_____ .
                                        6. living

_____ .
                                        7. fault

Roberta O'Reilly

2. **Mr. and Mrs. Taylor are applying for a loan from the bank. Use** *how much, why, how old, where,* *how many, how long* **and the banker's notes to complete the conversation.**

FIND OUT:

MR. TAYLOR'S JOB

THE AMOUNT OF TIME HE HAS WORKED THERE

THE AMOUNT OF MONEY HE EARNS

THE NUMBER OF LOANS THE TAYLOR'S HAVE ALREADY HAD

THE REASON FOR WANTING THE LOAN

HIS AGE

BANKER: Mr. Taylor, first of all, I need to know **where you work** and
              _____ there. Then you need to write here
                          2
              _____ .
                          3

MR. TAYLOR: We've only had one loan in the past five years, sir.

BANKER: Good. Write that here . . . Finally, you need to tell me _____
                                                                            4
              _____ and _____ .
                                              5

MR. TAYLOR: Do you want my yearly or monthly salary?

BANKER: Yearly salary please. Oh, yes, write here _____ .
                                                                6

MR. TAYLOR: Just me or my wife too?

BANKER: Just *your* age, Mr. Taylor.

3. **Unscramble the sentences.**

1. A: me tell where is can post office you the?

   Can you tell me where the post office is ?

   B: standing do see man where you is that?/right him it's behind.

   _____ . _____ ? _____ .

2. A: know the university far you how do is?

   _____ ?

   B: sure not is far I'm it how.

   _____ .

3. A: I often how know you have payment a make do to?

   _____ ?

   B: often not I'm sure how./maybe month a twice.

   _____ .

GERUNDS AS OBJECTS OF PREPOSITIONS

I'm interested in **writing** a book. She's bored with **cleaning** the house. We talked about **going** to California.	**I'm used to staying up late** means I'm accustomed to it. **I used to stay up late** means I did that before, but I don't do it anymore.

1. Fill in the blanks with infinitive phrases or gerund phrases.

ADVICE—All your questions answered

Dear Pamela

DEAR PAMELA:
I read the letter from "Puzzled in Kansas,"
and I wanted to write about my own experience.
Today my life is very different from

what it _used to be_ . When I lived
        _{1. used to/be}

with my parents, I was _____
              _{2. used to/do}

what my mother told me. I was afraid of

_____ her angry. I _____
_{3. make}   _{4. want/become}

_____ independent, but I didn't

know how. I was tired of _____ my
                _{5. be}

parents' slave, and I was worried about never

_____ any men. But
      _{6. get/know}

one day everything changed. I became fed up

with _____ my parents' little girl. I
     _{7. be}

_____ to a
        _{8. decided/move}

different city and become an independent
person. That was three years ago. Now I am
independent, and I'm not sorry about

_____ my family. I'm interested
     _{9. leave}

in _____ a doctor, and I'm
   _{10. become}

planning on _____ college soon.
       _{11. start}

    So tell "Puzzled" that she should let go of
her daughter. She'll be doing her a big favor.

                    —FREE IN TOPEKA

2. Complete the questions and circle your answers.

Will you be able to live happily in the future?   Take this test and see.

1. Are you excited about possibly _living_ on another planet?   Yes No
                         _{live}

2. Would you like to _____ all your work from a home computer   Yes No
                _{do}
    television system?

3. Are you used to _____ to recorded phone message receivers?   Yes No
                  _{talk}

4. Are you able to _____ your habits rapidly?   Yes No
                _{change}

5. Are you worried about _____ new kinds of food? Less meat?   Yes No
                   _{eat}
    More seaweed?

6. Are you afraid of _____ the changes in the future?   Yes No
               _{face}

3. Fill in the blanks in John's letter to Josie.

John J. Sullivan, Jr.
511 Maple Drive
Tulsa, Oklahoma

Dear Josie,

I read your ad in the Sunday paper. You said you were interested in *meeting* an
_____
1. meet

intelligent, attractive man in his 40's. Well, I'm your man! I'm very good at _____
2. make

conversation and _____ people to laugh. I'm fond of _____,
3. get   4. sail

_____, _____ and _____, but I also never
5. skydive   6. hike   7. parachute jump

tire of _____ at home quietly with someone I like.
8. sit

I'm planning on _____ in Oklahoma City on Friday on business. What do you say?
9. be

Let's meet for a drink. Don't be afraid of _____ yes to the best man to come your way
10. say

in years! I look forward to _____ from you.
11. hear

Yours truly,

John J.

4. Complete this part of a telephone conversation. Fill in the blanks with *used to* or *be used to*.

. . . . I'm calling about the ad in the paper . . . For a receptionist . . . Oh,

yes, lots of experience. I *used to* _____ work in a law office . . . No, that was
1

several years ago. After that I worked for a doctor and a . . . Of course, I don't mind

keeping late hours. I _____ putting in 10 or 12 hours of work a day. In fact, in my
2

last job, my boss _____ ask me to work on weekends too. So I
3

_____ giving all my time to my employer because . . . Next Monday?
4

Good, I'll be there . . . Don't worry about being late. I _____
5

waiting. I _____ have to wait for my old boss all the time. He
6

always . . . Excuse me? . . . Well, I'm a little nervous, that's true.

I _____ being interviewed by telephone.
(negative) 7

79

Our house **is** nice, **isn't it**?
You**'ll get** a raise soon, **won't you**?
You **weren't studying**, **were you**?
You **like** your job, **don't you**?
You **left** early, **didn't you**?

I**'m** really behind, **aren't I**?
You **don't like** me, **do you**?
He **can't come**, **can he**?
He **hasn't finished**, **has he**?
That noise **could be** the radiator, **couldn't it**?

Note:

If the main part of the tag question is affirmative, the tag is negative. If the main part of the tag question is negative, the tag is affirmative.

Speakers make the main part of the tag question affirmative when they expect an affirmative answer. She's nice, **isn't she? Yes, she is.**

1. **Complete the dialog between Mr. Brandon and his son Paul.**

MR. BRANDON: Paul, you want to become a doctor, *don't you* ₁?

PAUL: Yes, Dad.

MR. BRANDON: I've already paid a lot of money for your education, _____ ₂?

PAUL: Yes, you have.

MR. BRANDON: New England University is a good school, _____ ₃?

PAUL: Yes, it is.

MR. BRANDON: I'm supporting you, _____ ₄?

PAUL: Yes, you're supporting me.

MR. BRANDON: I give you plenty of money, _____ ₅?

PAUL: Dad, what's the . . .

MR. BRANDON: You studied for your exams, _____ ₆?

PAUL: Yes, I did.

MR. BRANDON: You're not unhappy, _____ ₇?

PAUL: Of course not.

MR. BRANDON: You haven't done anything wrong, _____ ₈?

PAUL: No, I don't think so.

MR. BRANDON: You can understand the material in your courses, _____ ₉?

PAUL: Yes, I can.

MR. BRANDON: Then why are your grades so terrible? You aren't in love, _____ ₁₀?

PAUL: Dad, what does love have to do with it?

2. **Match the sentences to make conversations, and fill in the blanks.**

1. I'm driving you crazy, *aren't* I?

2. John isn't home yet, _____ he?

3. He used to be a clerk, _____ he?

4. You want all the money, _____ you?

5. You don't really love me, _____ you?

6. Anita doesn't live here, _____ she?

a. No, she moved back to Phoenix.

b. Yes. Now he's a company manager.

c. Yes, I wish you'd calm down.

d. No, he called to say he'd be late.

e. Yes, I think I deserve it.

f. I like you, but I don't love you.

3. **Fill in the blanks to complete the questions and answers. Use the words given.**

Venus   Saturn   caves   Florida   1962   Greece

1. A: Tampa is in Georgia, *isn't it* ?

   B: No, _____ . It's in _____ .

2. A: Algeria used to be a French colony, _____ ?

   B: Yes, _____ . It became independent in _____ .

3. A: Jupiter doesn't have rings, _____ ?

   B: No, _____ . _____ has rings.

4. A: Rhodes and Crete are islands, _____ ?

   B: Yes, _____ . They're both off the coast of _____ .

5. A: Spelunkers explore the sea bottom, _____ ?

   B: No, _____ . They explore _____ .

6. A: The Russians have sent space probes to Mercury, _____ ?

   B: No, _____ . They've sent space probes to _____ .

4. **Complete the conversations.**

1. A: I'm not doing this right, *am I* ?

   B: Yes, you are. It's perfect.

2. A: You've been waiting for us a long time, _____ ?

   B: Not really. We just got here.

3. A: Your parents were living in Morocco when you were in school, _____ ?

   B: Yes, for part of the time.

4. A: Where should my friends stay in New York?

   B: They couldn't stay in your apartment, _____ ?

DEFINITE and INDEFINITE ARTICLES

> Are you going **to work** right now?
> No, not until ten-thirty.
>
> I'm interested in **the work** you do.
> I'll show it to you tomorrow.
>
> **The sun** is a star.
> Is it? I thought it was a planet.
>
> Are you going **to college** in the fall?
> Yes, I'm going **to Michigan State University**.
> That's **a huge school**.
> I know, but it has **the best** English department.
>
> Kathy is going **to the University of Kansas**.

1. Complete the sentences with *the* where appropriate. If no article is needed, put Ø.

1. A: Where are you going?

   B: To __Ø__ class. It starts at three.

2. A: Why are you smiling?

   B: This is _____ best class I've had.

3. A: I'm tired.

   B: Let's go to _____ bed.

4. A: Where does Billy sleep?

   B: His is _____ bed next to the door.

5. A: Where's Reverend Brown?

   B: He's at _____ jail with a new prisoner.

6. A: What happened to Bill?

   B: He was sent to _____ jail for 10 years.

7. A: Where does Kathy go to _____ school?

   B: At Midvale Elementary.

8. A: Dad, why is this picture here?

   B: That's _____ school I went to.

9. A: What shall we do today?

   B: Let's go to _____ town and shop.

10. A: Where did you live in Minnesota?

    B: In _____ only town on Gull Lake.

2. Write *a* or *the* where appropriate. Put Ø if an article is not needed.

You know, I put all six children through college. Amy attended __Ø__₁ Arizona State University.
It's _____₂ public university near Phoenix. Bill went to _____₃ University of Arizona. It's also
_____₄ public college, and it's _____₅ second largest university in _____₆ state of Arizona. Ben
and Howard went to _____₇ Columbia University. It's _____₈ private school in New York City. It's
one of _____₉ best schools in _____₁₀ East. Mark attended _____₁₁ College of Santa Fe. It's _____₁₂
small religious school in Santa Fe. My baby, Priscilla, went to _____₁₃ Oregon State, which
is _____₁₄ largest school in Oregon. What do you think of that? I never even finished high school!

Note:

Do not use the definite article with proper names of cities:
New York

Use the definite article with countries like:
the United States, the Soviet Union

Don't use the definite article with **breakfast,
lunch, dinner**.

3. **Disagree with the following statements. Write *a, an* or *the* in the blanks where appropriate.
Use the words given.**

Soviet Union   *star*   *sun's*

1. A: __The__ sun is __a__ planet.

   B: No, it isn't. It's _____ .

2. A: _____ moon shines by its own light.

   B: No, it doesn't. It shines by _____ light.

3. A: _____ United States is _____ largest country in _____ world.

   B: No, it isn't. _____ is the largest country in _____ world.

4. **Fill in the blanks with *a, an, the* or Ø.**

I had __a__ terrible day yesterday. I woke up at 5 o'clock in the morning and couldn't go
1

back to sleep, so I got up and started making _____ breakfast. I was trying to make _____
2   3

fried eggs, but _____ first thing I did was drop _____ egg on _____ floor. Finally I
4   5   6

finished breakfast and went to _____ work. It was raining so I decided to take _____ taxi.
7   8

_____ taxi driver charged me $6.00.
9

_____ work I was doing for Mrs. Peters was so boring. My friend and I were supposed to
10

go to _____ lunch at 12:00, but she couldn't go so I had _____ sandwich at my desk.
11   12

In the afternoon I worked on writing some reports and got _____ headache for all my
13

trouble. I left _____ work in _____ terrible mood. _____ bus going home was very
14   15   16

crowded.

When I got home, _____ dinner wasn't ready. My sister and I were supposed to go to a
17

movie at _____ university. We decided to go in her car, but then we couldn't get _____ car
18   19

started. Then it was too late, so we stayed home and listened to _____ records instead. What
20

a disappointing day.

Did you **wait for** Jim or leave? What's so funny?
We **waited for** him. I was **laughing at** the way you said that.

What should we do with all these things?
Get rid of them.

Note:

Some phrasal verbs have three parts—a main
verb and two other words:
get rid of   **take care of**   **get away with**

1. **Listen to Lucy describe her trip to Los Angeles. Complete the sentences using the verbs given.**

run into   wait for   look forward to   check into   check out of   listen to   pay for   laugh at

1. Here we are on the plane. Everybody was really

    looking forward to _____ the trip, but Mom was a

    little nervous.

2. Now we're _____ the hotel. The swimming

    pool was huge!

3. Here we are at Universal Studios. We're

    _____ a bus to start the tour.

4. We're _____ the tour guide explain how

    T.V. shows are made.

5. After Universal Studios we went to Disneyland. Here Dad is

    _____ our tickets.

6. Mom _____ an old college roommate from

    Santa Fe. They were so surprised to see each other.

7. Here we were all _____ the clown diver at

    Marineland.

8. Here's the last one. We're _____ the hotel

    and going back to Portland.

2. Complete the sentences to make conversations. Put the phrasal verbs in the right tense and add a pronoun.

1. A: Bill, let me treat you to lunch.

   B: No, I'm _paying for you_ .
      _{pay for}

2. A: What do you want to do about the problem?

   B: Let's _____ .
      _{talk about}

3. A: Have you seen Jerry lately?

   B: Yes. I _____ downtown today.
      _{run into}

4. A: Did the bus come on time?

   B: No, I had to _____ for about 45 minutes.
      _{wait for}

5. A: Are you worried about Mary?

   B: Yes. I _____ all the time.
      _{think about}

3. James Gibson is running for mayor of South Falls. Read the interview and fill in the blanks with phrasal verbs and any necessary pronouns.

Run into/get away from

INTERVIEWER: Mr. Gibson, what will you do if you become mayor?

GIBSON: The first thing is to balance the budget. We need to _get away from_ spending
         ₁
         money we don't have. If we don't, we're going to _____ real trouble.
         ₂

Cut down on/run out of

INTERVIEWER: Mr. Gibson, will oil continue to be a problem?

GIBSON: Yes, we're _____ very fast. We have to find other kinds of
        ₃
        energy and _____ our present use of oil.
        ₄

Look forward to/look up to

INTERVIEWER: How do you feel about the next debate with the present mayor?

GIBSON: I'm _____ .
        ₅

INTERVIEWER: Mr. Gibson, a government official should be respected. Do you think the people

        _____ ?
        ₆

GIBSON: Yes, I feel I have their trust.

85

PHRASAL VERBS—*Separable*

> Where's the garbage?
> I **took** it **out** already.
>
> What time did you **get up** this morning?
> Well, the rain **woke** me **up** at 5 A.M., but I didn't **get up** until 8:00.
>
> Can we **put** the dinner **off** until next week?
> Sure.

1. Use the pictures and the correct forms of the verbs given to complete the sentences.

clean up   get up   wake up   take off   move out   move in   call up   pick up

1. John **woke up** at 5 A.M. again.

2. He didn't _____ until 7:00. He wanted some time to think.

3. He realized he wasn't happy at home anymore. He wanted to

    _____.

Later that day . . .

4. They said that Flight #301 was ready for boarding. John

    _____ his jacket, fastened his seat belt and

    _____ a magazine. He felt better already.

Three months later . . .

5. John rented this cabin a month ago. Now he's

    _____.

6. The cabin is really dirty, so he's _____.

7. He's at home now—and happy. He's _____ his parents

    just to say hello.

Note:

These phrasal verbs can be separated or not when they are followed by a *noun*:
I **took** the *garbage* **out**. OR I **took out** the *garbage*.

These verbs must always be separated when they are used with a *pronoun*:
I **took** *it* **out**.

2. **Complete the conversations with one of the verbs given and a pronoun.**

figure out   call off   turn on   wake up   put out   try on   call up

1. A: It's late. What shall I do about José?
   B: ___*Wake him up*___ .

2. A: I want Yoko to come to the movies with us.
   B: _____ .

3. A: I don't know how much wood I need
      to build the bookcase.
   B: _____ .

4. A: I want to listen to the radio.
   B: _____ .

5. A: I don't want to have this party after all.
   B: _____ .

6. A: I don't know whether these pants will fit me.
   B: _____ .

7. A: What shall I do with my cigarette?
   B: _____ .

3. **Complete Mike's diary entry with phrasal verbs. Use pronouns if needed.**

figure out   find out   try out   take out   call up   fill up   pick up   break up

June 10

Yesterday I ___*found out*___ something awful. Jane and I had a date to go to the
                  1

movies. I _____ at noon to ask what time I should _____ . She
             2   3

said she wasn't feeling well and asked if we could skip the movie. I was disappointed but I said

of course, if she felt that bad. Last night I decided to _____ Bill's new motorcycle. I
                                                              4

_____ of the garage, _____ the tank and went out for a ride.
        5   6

When I was at a traffic light, I looked at the car next to me. There was Jane with another guy. I

can't _____ . Why did she lie to me? If she wanted to _____ ,
            7   8

why didn't she say so?

I'm happy, and **so is** Carla. I like our new home, and **so does** she.
We moved last year, and **so did** my brother.
I didn't like our old house, and **neither did** Carla.
I'm not sorry, and **neither is** she.

Note:

Use **so** to connect two affirmative statements.
Use **neither** to connect two negative statements.

1. **Match the sentences to make conversations. Use *so* and *neither* to fill in the blanks.**

1. I hate disco music.
2. I don't like steak.
3. Hiroko doesn't like Takeo.
4. I used to smoke.
5. Tony wasn't in class today.
6. Bruno should go on a diet.

a. _____, but I finally quit.

b. _____ Nelson. They're sick.

c. _____ Pietro. He looks fat.

d. *So do I* _____. It sounds like noise.

e. _____. I don't eat meat.

f. _____ Akiko. He's too pushy.

2. **Sue and Harry Wilkins recently moved to Victoria. Mr. Wilkins and Bob Bradley are talking about it. Fill in the dialog with *so* or *neither* plus a subject and a verb.**

HARRY: I like Victoria, and *so does Mary* . I don't miss Toronto, and _____
                1. Mary

_____ .
2. she

BOB: What do you like about it?

HARRY: Well, the climate is great, and _____ . Food isn't too expensive,
                                      3. people

and _____ . I got an almost new car for a great
                 4. the heating bills

price. Houses aren't that expensive here. I couldn't afford a house in Toronto, and _____

_____ when he lived there. Here I can.
                 5. my brother

BOB: What about all the cultural advantages of Toronto? Don't you miss them?

HARRY: Not really. For example, I didn't care that much for the theater, and _____

_____ . We're happy in Victoria.
      6. Mary

3. **Unscramble the sentences.**

1. early, Jim up get hates to does and so Helen.

   Jim *hates to get up early, and so does Helen* .

2. to I telephone, Susan on neither and the like doesn't do talk.

   Susan _____ .

3. less I should you and so eat should.

   You _____ .

4. has I to neither Rio, and Stan been haven't.

   I _____ .

5. summer, Martha would go Hawaii to I'd and so this like to.

   I'd _____ .

4. **Tim Lucas is on a quiz program. Write his answers using *so* or *neither*.**

QUIZMASTER: Lions are carnivores. Tigers?

TIM: *So are tigers* .
                    1

QUIZMASTER: The Americans have landed on the moon. The Russians?

TIM: _____ .
                    2

QUIZMASTER: China is a member of the United Nations. England?

TIM: _____ .
                    3

QUIZMASTER: Spain fought a civil war. The United States?

TIM: _____ .
                    4

QUIZMASTER: Chicago has more than two million people. Los Angeles?

TIM: _____ .
                    5

QUIZMASTER: Cubans don't speak Portuguese. Venezuelans?

TIM: _____ .
                    6

QUIZMASTER: India used to be a British colony. Nigeria?

TIM: _____ .
                    7

QUIZMASTER: Napoleon wasn't English. Madame Curie?

TIM: _____ .
                    8

QUIZMASTER: Russia hasn't landed on Jupiter. America?

TIM: _____ .
                    9

> I **feel** good.
> The flowers **smell** wonderful.
> Carla **looks** beautiful.
>
> The food **tastes** delicious.
> That music **sounds** nice.

Note:

Use adjectives, not adverbs, after verbs of perception:
feel, **look**, **smell**, **taste** and **sound**.

1. Giorgio is telling Nicola his troubles. Fill in the blanks with sense verbs and adjectives.

GIORGIO: Nicola, yesterday morning the world _**looked good**_ . The flowers

_____ . My wife _____ . Breakfast
2. smell sweet   3. look beautiful

_____ . I _____ . I heard songs on the radio
4. taste delicious   5. feel energetic

and they _____ . . . . Today, well, everything is different.
6. sound wonderful

The world _____ . The flowers _____ . My wife
7. look ugly   8. look tired

_____ . I _____ . Every song I hear
9. look worn out   10. feel depressed

_____ .
11. sound terrible

NICOLA: That happens to everybody, Giorgio. Things will _____ tomorrow.
12. look better

2. Complete the statements.

1. A: I thought the orchestra played _**beautifully**_ .
      beautiful

   B: I thought they sounded _**terrible**_ .
      terrible

2. A: This time I followed the recipe very _____ .
      careful

   B: Yeah, you must have. It smells _____ .
      delicious

3. A: The boys have been painting _____ all morning.
      quiet

   B: I can see that. Their pictures look _____ .
      beautiful

4. A: Ken worked very _____ on the project for days.
      hard

   B: That's why he feels _____ .
      terrible

5. A: Mrs. Carter tends her garden so _____ .
      loving

   B: Yeah, she does. The roses smell especially _____ .
      sweet

3. Write sentences with sense verbs about what's happening in the pictures. Choose the best adjective given.

1. Mr. Brown _looked unhappy_ .
   sour/unhappy

2. Mr. Garcia _____ .
   beautiful/happy

3. The soup _____ .
   happy/delicious

4. The milk _____ .
   sour/bitter

5. The music _____ .
   delicious/wonderful

6. The music _____ .
   bitter/horrible

7. The food _____ .
   terrible/unhappy

8. The food _____ .
   sweet/delicious

9. Yesterday Ken _____ .
   tired/horrible

10. Today he _____ .
    fine/delicious

4. Answer the questions using sense verbs. Use the adjectives given. Some can be used more than once.

angry   sweet   sour   tired   bitter   terrible

1. A: How do roses usually smell?

   B: _They usually smell sweet_ .

2. A: How does a person with a cold usually feel?

   B: _____ .

3. A: How does spoiled milk smell?

   B: _____ .

4. A: How does honey taste?

   B: _____ .

5. A: How do lemons taste?

   B: _____ .

6. A: How does a person who has worked all day usually look?

   B: _____ .

7. A: How do people having an argument sound?

   B: _____ .

91

> Some people like small cars.
> **Other** people like big cars.
> **Others** prefer to walk.
>
> Only three students came today.
> **One** student is on vacation.
> All **the others** are sick.
>
> I'll have **another** Coke please.
>
> My husband and I love **each other**.
>
> Where are **the other** children?
> They're at the beach.

1. **Complete the dialogs with *one*, *another* and *the other*.**

DEALER: Pick four cards and put them face down on the table.

PLAYER: OK.

DEALER: Pick up __One__ of them; now
1

pick up _____ one; now
2

_____ one. Now pick up
3

_____ one.
4

PLAYER: I've got 15 points. I lose.

MOTHER: Take out three eggs. Put _____ in
5

a bowl and beat it up.

SUZY: How long?

MOTHER: A minute . . . then add a cup of sugar.

Beat in _____ egg and
6

then take _____ one
7

and separate the yolk from the white.
Then fold the white into

_____ eggs.
8

BOSS: Where did you put the last three packages?

MAIL BOY: I left _____ in the mail room, I
9

took _____ one to
10

Mr. James' office and I left

_____ one on the table.
11

BOSS: So where's the _____
12

you left on the table?

MAIL BOY: I don't know.

BIRD WATCHER 1: Do you see any birds?

BIRD WATCHER 2: I sure do. I see three.

BIRD WATCHER 1: Well, what are they?

BIRD WATCHER 2: _____'s an egret.
13

_____ is a heron
14

and . . . wow, . . .

_____ one's an eagle!
15

2. Complete the conversations with *the other* or *the others*.

1. A: Do you want these bananas?

   B: No, I want _the others_. They're on sale.

2. A: Is this the book you need?

   B: No, I need _____ one—the one on the table.

3. A: I really like these roses.

   B: I do too. But I like _____ ones better.

4. A: Here are your groceries, Mrs. La Madrid.

   B: But this is only half the order. Where are _____ things?

3. Write *other* or *others* in the blanks.

1. A: Do you like soap operas?

   B: I think some are OK. _Others_ are pretty bad.

2. A: Do you think American cars are good?

   B: Some are. _____ are lemons.

3. A: Where is everybody?

   B: Heather and Erica went to the beach. The _____ kids went to the movies.

4. A: These pants are too tight.

   B: The _____ are on the chair. Try them.

4. Put *another, the other, other* or *each other* in this letter to Pamela.

ADVICE—All your questions answered

Dear Pamela

DEAR PAMELA:
I have a problem that I'm not sure you can solve. I've been going out with Jack for ten years now. But I'm also in love with

another man. We can't stand
   1.

to be away from _____ .
                     2.

I love Jack, but this _____ love is
                         3.

very powerful. I've talked to _____
                                  4.

women about this. They all say I should stay with Jack. What do you think?

—BEWILDERED

DEAR BEWILDERED:
Of course, they're right. If you love your boyfriend, as you say, you don't need

_____ man in your life. If
   5.

you and Jack love _____ ,
                      6.

you should stay together. Your friends know what is best for you. Listen to them.

> What **caused** the accident?
> The driver was speeding.
> What time **did** it **happen**?
> At 11:30.
>
> Who **did** you **see**?
> Three policemen.
> Who **saw** you?
> Nobody.

1. Write questions to complete the dialogs.

1. BRENDA: _What happened to your leg_ ?
   <small>what/happen to your leg</small>

   ALICE: I broke it skiing.

   BRENDA: _____ ?
   <small>how/do it</small>

   ALICE: I ran into a snowbank and couldn't stop.

2. GWEN: _____ ?
   <small>who/live in that ugly old house</small>

   ED: Mrs. Crone does.

   GWEN: _____ ?
   <small>why/live in such an ugly place</small>

   ED: She can't afford to live anywhere else.

3. BILL: _____ ? It's fantastic.
   <small>who/take/this picture</small>

   ALAN: I did.

   BILL: _____ ?
   <small>when/take it</small>

   ALAN: Last summer at the lake.

2. Fill in the blanks to make questions. Use *do, did* or *does* when the question word replaces the object. Do not use them when it replaces the subject.

1. A: _How far did you travel_ on your vacation?
   <small>you/travel</small>

   B: Last year? About 2,500 miles.

2. A: _____ your parents?
   <small>you/see</small>

   B: About four times a year.

3. A: _____ with the car?
   <small>go wrong</small>

   B: The battery went dead.

4. A: _____ with?
   <small>Mary/live</small>

   B: Her Aunt Edith.

5. A: _____ ?
   <small>the play/start</small>

   B: Eight o'clock. We'd better get going.

3. **Complete the following dialogs by writing questions.**

POLICE CHIEF: This man died at 1:10 A.M. He was murdered.

REPORTER 1: *How did he die* ?
1. how/die

REPORTER 2: _____ ?
2. who/kill

FIRE CHIEF: This fire did not start by accident.

REPORTER 1: _____ ?
3. who/start

REPORTER 2: _____ ?
4. when/start

DOCTOR: Mrs. Hancock died from something she ate. She was poisoned.

REPORTER 1: _____ ?
5. who/poison

REPORTER 2: _____ ?
6. what/eat

REPORTER 3: _____ ?
7. what time/die

TOUR GUIDE: Some very wealthy people lived in this old mansion.

TOURIST 1: _____ ?
8. who/live

TOURIST 2: _____ ?
9. how long/live

TOURIST 3: _____ ?
10. what/happen

4. **You are on a T.V. quiz show called DANGER. Make up the questions for these answers.**

Answers

1. Columbus. *Who discovered America* ?
   discover America

2. Shakespeare. _____ ?
   Romeo and Juliet

3. 5,280. _____ ?
   feet in a mile

4. 1776. _____ ?
   the American Revolution begin

5. Tegucigalpa. _____ ?
   the capital of Honduras

6. 80 miles. _____ ?
   New York from Philadelphia

7. A volcano. _____ ?
   destroy Pompeii

I **love** Paris.	I'**ve been** here for over a week.
I'**m having** a wonderful time.	I'**ll leave** next week.
I **arrived** here last Tuesday.	I'**m going** to go to England next.
I **was planning** to arrive on Wednesday.	

1. **Fill in the blanks in Susan's letter to her mother. Use the correct tense of the indicated verb.**

Dear Mom,

I *'ve been* _____ in Paris for a week now and I _____ it.
  1. be   2. love

I _____ sightseeing several times. I _____ to the Eiffel Tower
    3. already be   4. go

yesterday afternoon and to Montmartre the day before that. Later this afternoon I

_____ the Louvre. Tomorrow morning I _____ Barbara at the train
    5. visit   6. meet

station. On Thursday we _____ a train to Berlin. We _____ back in
        7. take   8. not be

St. Paul until the middle of July. I _____ a wonderful time, really, and the
        9. have

best thing is that I _____ all my money yet.
    10. not spend

Give my love to everybody. I _____ you about July 20th.
        11. see

Love, *Susan*

2. **Complete the dialogs by disagreeing. Put *too* or *either* and the right verb in the blanks.**

1. A: I didn't sleep at all last night.

   B: *You did too* . I heard you snoring.

2. A: I was awake at three A.M.

   B: _____ . _____ sound asleep.

3. A: Bonnie has never met Joe.

   B: _____ . _____ last summer.

4. A: You don't love me.

   B: _____ . _____ a lot.

5. A: Greg was late again today.

   B: _____ . _____ here at 9:00.

6. A: Ah ha! I caught you. You weren't studying.

   B: _____ . _____ memorizing the important dates.

3. **Use the cues to write questions on Professor Wilson's history test. Then circle *Yes* or *No*.**

1. *Was Kennedy president from 1952–1956* _____ ?   Yes   (No)
   _{Kennedy/be/president/from 1952–1956}

2. _____ ?   Yes   No
   _{the U.S. president/live/in the White House}

3. _____ ?   Yes   No
   _{World War I/last/from 1914–1918}

4. _____ ?   Yes   No
   _{China/be/a member of the United Nations/since 1973}

5. _____ ?   Yes   No
   _{the first men/land/on the moon/in 1949}

6. _____ ?   Yes   No
   _{Nigeria/be/a British Colony}

7. _____ ?   Yes   No
   _{the Chinese/send people into space/for years}

4. **Fill in the blanks in Dora's diary. Use the correct tense of the indicated verbs.**

Dear Diary,

Today __*was*__ a day to remember. It _____ normally. I _____ at the
   1. be   2. start   3. get up

usual time, _____ breakfast and _____ cleaning the house. While I
           4. have   5. start

_____ the rug, the phone _____ . I _____ it, and a
    6. vacuum   7. ring   8. answer

voice _____, "_____ this Dora Gomez?"
    9. say   10. be

"Yes," I _____.
       11. say

"Your father _____ in an accident. Can you come to Memorial Hospital right away?"
          12. be

"Of course. I _____ right there. Is he all right?"
         13. be

"Yes," _____ the voice. "But hurry."
       14. say

I _____ into my Volkswagen and _____ to the hospital. But when I
      15. jump   16. drive

_____ there, no one _____ anything about my father.
   17. get   18. know

When I _____ back home, guess what I _____ ? My television and my stereo
       19. get   20. find

_____ gone! The whole thing _____ a trick to get me out of the house. I
   21. be   22. be

_____ the police and _____ the crime. I can't believe it!
   23. call   24. report

Answer Key

Unit One

1.   1. were eating/True 2. were walking/True 3. was driving/True 4. was teaching/False 5. was checking/True 6. were watching/True 7. were having/False

2.   1. were you driving/wasn't/was/going 2. was Mary thinking/wasn't/was/joking 3. were you living/weren't/were/staying 4. were you studying/wasn't/was studying

3.   1. were you driving 2. were you going 3. was it raining 4. Was anyone sitting 5. Was he wearing 6. Were you wearing

4.   1. I wasn't/I was/resting 2. it wasn't/It was/raining 3. they weren't/They were speaking 4. he wasn't/He was singing 5. you weren't/You were eating

Unit Two

1.   1. the telephone rang/I was making dinner 2. the volcano erupted/People were hiking up the mountain 3. a burglar broke into the house/Mr. and Mrs. Ramirez were watching T.V. 4. her car had a flat tire/Samantha was driving down the street

2.   1. was jumping 2. was chasing 3. was painting 4. were playing 5. was cutting 6. crawled 7. climbed 8. hid

3.   1. happen/was waiting 2. were making/burned 3. were watching/broke out 4. saw/was running 5. came/was wrapping

4.   1. woke up 2. was shining 3. got up 4. did 5. was doing 6. rang 7. was calling 8. wanted 9. was getting dressed 10. rang 11. wanted 12. ran 13. jumped 14. drove 15. wasn't (was not) shining 16. was waiting 17. ran into 18. knocked 19. got out 20. ran

Unit Three

1.   1. a record player 2. a song writer 3. window washers 4. bus drivers 5. a house painter

2.   1. It's a ten-story building. 2. It's a ten-foot pole. 3. It's a two-hour flight. 4. They're fifty-pound bags. 5. It's a two-hour trip. 6. It's an eight hundred-page book. 7. It's a 34-inch belt. 8. They're ten-gallon tanks.

Unit Four

1.   1. e/Could 2. b/could/couldn't 3. d/couldn't 4. a/couldn't 5. c/could

2.   1. Can you remember 2. Could you see 3. could see 4. couldn't hear 5. Could you understand 6. could understand 7. can't think 8. could smell 9. can remember

Unit Five

1.   1. Aren't/mammals 2. Isn't/a kingdom 3. Wasn't/neutral 4. Wasn't/a scientist 5. Weren't/Egyptians

2.   1. Isn't 2. Aren't 3. No 4. Aren't 5. Isn't 6. Yes 7. Aren't 8. No 9. Isn't 10. Yes

Unit Six

1.   1. Can't you 2. Can't they 3. Can't he 4. Can't you 5. Can't he

2.   1. Can't 2. Can't 3. Couldn't 4. Couldn't

Unit Seven

1.   1. c/Doesn't it 2. a/Didn't you 3. d/Don't you 4. e/Didn't I 5. f/Don't 6. b/Didn't you

2.   1. Didn't you 2. Don't you 3. Didn't you 4. Don't you 5. Don't you

3.   1. Don't/live/Asia 2. Doesn't/costs over $15,000 3. Didn't/started/1939

Unit Eight

1.   1. can I 2. Can she 3. Can we (Can I) 4. Can we (Can I) 5. Can I 6. Can we 7. Can we (Can I)

2.   1. b 2. d 3. c 4. a

Unit Nine

1.   1. wanted to save 2. agreed to have 3. refused to feel 4. decided to do 5. planned to run 6. hoped to raise 7. promised to continue 8. offered to support

2.   1. Does/need to 2. Does/have to 3. Do/like to 4. Does/have to 5. Do/want to 6. Does/have to

3.   1. I like to go dancing. 2. I don't like to cook. *Answers will be students' own likes and dislikes.*

Unit Ten

1 1. to do 2. to mow 3. to clean up 4. to do 5. to make 6. to wash 7. to pick up 8. to feed

2 1. She told her to 2. She didn't tell her to 3. She told her to 4. She didn't tell her to 5. She told her to 6. She didn't tell her to 7. She told her to 8. She didn't tell her to

3 1. do you want me to do 2. do you want me to type 3. wants you to do 4. like you to type 5. ask her to check 6. ask him to come in 7. want him to help

4 1. Did you ask the Millers to come to dinner? 2. Yes, I asked them to come tonight. 3. Does Alice want me to come to the party? 4. Of course she wants you to come.

Unit Eleven

1 1. b/have to 2. c/like to 3. a/want to 4. d/needs to

2 1. asked him to 2. told her to 3. don't/want her to 4. didn't/want him to 5. asked them to 6. didn't tell him to

Unit Twelve

1 1. hard 2. fast (well) 3. well 4. fast 5. well 6. hard

2 1. How hard 2. How fast 3. how well (how fast) 4. How well 5. How hard

Unit Thirteen

1 1. very small 2. very big 3. very tall 4. very short 5. very old 6. very young 7. very expensive 8. very cheap

2 1. b/too much 2. f/too expensive 3. d/too many 4. e/too nice 5. c/too sweet 6. a/too short

3 1. too expensive 2. very expensive 3. very late 4. too late 5. very fast 6. too fast

4 1. very 2. too much 3. too many 4. very 5. too much 6. too many 7. very

Unit Fourteen

1 1. carelessly 2. carefully 3. quickly 4. slowly 5. happily 6. sadly 7. well 8. badly

2 1. How well does he drive/Very well and very carefully 2. How fast does she type/Very fast and very accurately 3. How well does he write/Very well and very quickly 4. How fluently does she speak Russian/Very fluently

3 1. well 2. fast 3. carefully 4. badly 5. gladly 6. hard 7. eagerly 8. eagerly 9. terribly 10. well 11. quickly

4 1. Did you do well on the test?/No, I did terribly. 2. Sara drove into the garage very slowly (Sara drove very slowly into the garage)./She ran over my bicycle. 3. Doctor, how is my husband doing?/He's resting comfortably. 4. You play beautifully./I enjoy it. 5. She speaks English fluently./She studies very hard.

Unit Fifteen

1 1. Does he have enough/No 2. Does she have enough/No 3. Does he have enough/Yes 4. Does she have enough/No

2 1. good enough 2. smart enough 3. enough patience 4. long enough 5. enough space

Unit Sixteen

1 1. too 2. enough 3. too 4. enough 5. enough 6. too 7. too 8. enough

2 1. Too tired 2. enough energy 3. too late 4. enough time 5. too much 6. too rushed

Unit Seventeen

1 1. Nothing 2. Everyone (Everybody) 3. Nowhere 4. No one (Nobody) 5. anywhere 6. Everywhere

2 1. Everything 2. somewhere 3. somewhere 4. anywhere 5. everyone (everybody) 6. anyone (anybody) 7. something 8. everything 9. someone (somebody) 10. nothing 11. everytime 12. someone (somebody) 13. anytime 14. sometime

3 1. Everyone/someone 2. anything/something

4 **Across:** 1. nowhere 6. have 7. as 9. one 10. Ed 12. th 13. everywhere 14. Is 16. None 17. place 19. we 20. Al 21. anybody **Down:** 1. no one 2. where 3. ha 4. everyone 5. red 8. someone 11. these 12. thing 15. ill 17. pan 18. can 19. wav

Unit Eighteen

1 1. Have you ever been 2. haven't done 3. you've been 4. 've never gone 5. Have you seen 6. Have you ever driven 7. haven't

2 1. I've never met her. 2. I've never been there. 3. We've never talked about it. 4. I've never flown in one. 5. You've never discussed it with me.

3 1. Have you seen 2. Have you ever read 3. have you ever told/'ve never told 4. Has Don ever done 5. Have they eaten

4 1. Sam Sacks has written two poems recently. He published *Electra* in April and *Songs of Life* in May. 2. Luis Santana has received two awards recently. He got the Oustanding Citizen of Wobegon and the R.C. Fields Award. 3. Alice Smith has run in six races in the past three months. She took first place in the Boston Marathon in May. 4. Bill and Gladys Stone have gone on three safaris recently. They went to Kenya in January, Ethiopia in February and India in April. 5. Eli Svartvik has made two short films in the past six months. He finished *Bombay* in January and *The Last World* in May.

Unit Nineteen

1 1. For 2. Since 3. For 4. Since

2 1. have known 2. got 3. have lived 4. has worked 5. has worked 6. have been 7. had

3 1. How long have you been married 2. How long have you worked 3. How long has she taught 4. How long have you lived 5. Have you owned

4 1. Frank has lived in Toronto since 1973 (for 11 years). 2. He has worked at Minnetonka Elementary School since 1974 (for ten years). 3. He has been principal of the school since 1980 (for four years). 4. Frank and Susan have known each other since 1975 (for nine years). 5. They have been married since 1978 (for six years). 6. They have had their house since 1981 (for three years). 7. They have owned their property in the country since 1983 (for one year).

Unit Twenty

1 1. 've been living 2. 's been working 3. 's been working 4. 's been studying 5. 's been studying 6. 've been going

2 1. have you been smoking 2. has she been wearing 3. have you been doing 4. have Jim and Nancy been dating 5. has she been playing 6. have we been talking

3 1. he's been writing 2. she's been reading 3. 've been constructing 4. 's been painting 5. She's been making 6. They've been taking 7. he's been building 8. she's been typing

Unit Twenty-One

1 1. He has climbed the Statue of Liberty. 2. He hasn't visited the World Trade Center. 3. He hasn't seen a Broadway play. 4. He has eaten in Greenwich Village. 5. He has visited the United Nations. 6. He hasn't gone to Central Park. 7. He has gone shopping at Macy's. 8. He hasn't ridden the subways.

2 1. Has Jim finished 2. Has Robin gotten out of 3. Have you done 4. Have you sold 5. Have we gone 6. have you seen

3 1. he's had administrative experience 2. I've worked in advertising 3. we haven't seen *The Big Chill* 4. she's worked with couples and small groups 5. He's worked in Mexico

4 1. have you written 2. I've written 3. I finished 4. you've lived 5. left 6. you travelled 7. spent 8. you've done 9. I hunted 10. I climbed 11. I was 12. did you do

Unit Twenty-Two

1 1. It used to be very peaceful, but it isn't anymore. 2. She used to be quite heavy, but she isn't anymore. 3. They used to be really rude, but they aren't anymore. 4. He used to get angry a lot, but he doesn't anymore. 5. They used to be very silly, but they aren't anymore.

2 1. There used to be/there's 2. There didn't use to be/there is (there's) 3. There used to be/there are 4. There didn't use to be/there are

Unit Twenty-Three

1 1. a little 2. a few 3. a few 4. a little 5. a little 6. a few 7. a few 8. a little

2 1. c/a little 2. d/a few 3. a/a little 4. b/a few 5. f/a few 6. e/a little

Unit Twenty-Four

1 1. How much do you need 2. How many does she speak 3. How many do you need 4. How much did she borrow 5. How much does it cost 6. How many does she have

2 1. much 2. much 3. many 4. much

3 1. She doesn't have many friends. 2. I don't have much time to finish this. 3. I didn't see many people I knew. 4. We don't have much fun at big parties. 5. There isn't much excitement there. 6. There aren't many children nearby. 7. There aren't many calories in an apple.

4 (5) We sure have a lot of homework. (2) I know. I've been having a lot of trouble doing the exercises. (1) Have you? They really aren't that difficult. You just need a lot of time to concentrate. (4) Time to concentrate? But I have too much to do already. (3) Yeah, me too. Well, good luck. See you tomorrow.

Unit Twenty-Five

1 1. Most of 2. Some of/some of 3. All of/None of 4. All of/A few of

2 1. c/A few 2. b/a few 3. a/All of 4. f/None of 5. d/Most 6. e/some of

3 1. All of 2. passed 3. A few of 4. got 5. most of 6. got 7. Some of 8. missed 9. some of

4 1. some/a few 2. none of/Some of/some 3. Most of/All of/Most of

Unit Twenty-Six

1 wider/bigger/narrower/taller/thinner/sillier/nicer/cheaper/happier

2 1. bigger 2. tastier than 3. easier 4. cheaper 5. healthier 6. happier 7. sweeter 8. saltier 9. prettier 10. thinner 11. tighter 12. slower 13. sicker than

3 1. The Sahara Desert is bigger than the Mojave Desert. 2. Jojo is heavier than Pete. 3. Marianne is taller than Sue. 4. Mt. Everest is taller than Mt. Kilimanjaro.

4 1. Which is cheaper 2. cheaper/than 3. Which is safer 4. safer 5. Which are friendlier 6. friendlier/than 7. Which are cleaner 8. cleaner 9. duller 10. duller 11. easier

Unit Twenty-Seven

1 1. better 2. more 3. farther 4. better 5. worse 6. less

2 1. Which is farther 2. Which/less 3. Which/more 4. Which is farther 5. Which/is worse 6. Which is better 7. Which is better

Unit Twenty-Eight

1 1. more interesting than 2. more important 3. more exciting than 4. more crowded 5. more dangerous 6. more expensive 7. more peaceful 8. more polite 9. more respectful than 10. more satisfying than

2 1. Which/is more exciting 2. Which is more interesting 3. Which/is more difficult 4. Which/are more interesting 5. Is/more demanding than 6. was more demanding 7. more fun

Unit Twenty-Nine

1 1. the shortest/False 2. the tallest/True 3. the largest/True 4. the smallest/True

2 1. What is the nicest part of the city to stay in 2. What is the cheapest hotel to stay at 3. What is the fastest way to travel around

3 1. _____ is the prettiest city I've ever seen. 2. _____ is the ugliest city I've ever been to. 3. _____ is the nicest city I've ever been in. 4. _____ is the oldest city I've ever been in. *Answers will be students' own opinions.*

Unit Thirty

1 the biggest/the most important/the tallest/the oldest/the most crowded/the most expensive/the most dangerous/the friendliest/the most interesting/the cheapest/the prettiest/the most exciting/the richest/the most intelligent/the most beautiful

2 1. the most crowded 2. the least crowded 3. the most dangerous 4. the least dangerous

3 1. I think _____ is the most beautiful city in _____ . 2. I think _____ is the least beautiful city in _____ . 3. I think _____ is the most important city in _____ . 4. I think _____ is the most interesting place in _____ . 5. I think _____ is the most

(continued)

exciting place in _____. **6.**I think _____ is the most dangerous sport. **7.**I think _____ is the most expensive entertainment. *Answers will be students' own opinions.*

Unit Thirty-One

1 **1.**the best **2.**the worst **3.**the most **4.**the least **5.**the farthest

2 **1.**the best **2.**the best **3.**the best **4.**the most **5.**the farthest **6.**the least **7.**the worst

Unit Thirty-Two

1 **1.**as happy as **2.**as good as **3.**as expensive as **4.**as big as **5.**as hard as **6.**as friendly as

2 **1.**n't as good as **2.**as tall as **3.**not as important as **4.**as smart as

Unit Thirty-Three

1 **1.**the same size **2.**They're the same age **3.**They make the same amount **4.**They're the same height **5.**They're the same distance

2 **1.**the same height as/taller than **2.**the same length as/longer than **3.**the same size as/smaller than **4.**the same amount/as/less than

Unit Thirty-Four

1 **1.**as much money/as **2.**doesn't/as much money/as **3.**don't/as many cars as **4.**isn't/as much as (as many courses as) **5.**doesn't/as many people as

2 **1.**as many friends **2.**as many problems **3.**as much money as **4.**as much fun **5.**as much trouble as **6.**as many cigarettes as

Unit Thirty-Five

1 **1.**less **2.**fewer **3.**more **4.**more

2 **1.**I have fewer problems than I used to. **2.**I earn less money than my son does. **3.**I'm taking fewer subjects this semester than last. **4.**Bill has more friends than he used to.

3 **1.**Well, there's less than there used to be. **2.**There are fewer than there used to be. **3.**There are fewer than there used to be. **4.**There's less than there used to be.

Unit Thirty-Six

1 **1.**India has the most people per square mile **2.**The Soviet Union has the fewest people per square mile **3.**The Soviet Union has the most land **4.**India has the least land **5.**The Soviet Union has the most reserves of mercury **6.**India has the fewest reserves of mercury **7.**China has the most trade **8.**India has the least trade

2 **1.**the fewest **2.**the least **3.**the fewest **4.**the most

Unit Thirty-Seven

1 **1.**the longest/longer than/as long as **2.**the highest/lower/as low as

2 **1.**works more quickly than Bob. **2.**speaks more intelligently too. **3.**responded the most enthusiastically. **4.**never acted more stupidly. **5.**speak Portuguese as well as I do.

Unit Thirty-Eight

1 **1.**should we do **2.**Should I make **3.**Let's go out **4.**Why don't we go **5.**let's not go **6.**Let's go

2 **1.**b/Let's/let's not **2.**d/Should we/let's **3.**a/should we/Let's **4.**f/Should I **5.**c/Should we (I)/let's not **6.**e/Should we

3 **1.**Let's not **2.**Let's **3.**let's not **4.**Why don't we **5.**Let's **6.**Let's not **7.**Why don't we

Unit Thirty-Nine

1 **1.**would like to live (would rather live)/True **2.**would rather live (would like to live)/True **3.**would rather live (would like to live)/True **4.**would like to rent (would rather rent)/True **5.**would rather buy (would like to buy)/True **6.**would like to have (would rather have)/False **7.**would rather have (would like to have)/False **8.**would rather have (would like to have)/True **9.**would like to buy (would rather buy)/True **10.**would like to buy (would rather buy)/True **11.**would like to buy (would rather buy)/True

2 **1.**would you like **2.**I'd like **3.**would you rather **4.**I'd rather **5.**I'd rather not **6.**How about **7.**They'd like **8.**How about

3 1. Would you rather/I'd rather be _____ .
2. Would you like/Would you rather/I'd rather
_____ . 3. Would you rather/I'd rather
_____ . 4. would you rather/I'd rather
_____ . 5. would you like/I'd like to _____ .
Answers will be students' own opinions.

Unit Forty

1 1. 'll be 2. will be 3. will Dad be 4. will you get
5. won't make 6. 'll spend 7. 'll get 8. 'll see
2 1. Will we have another world war 2. Will we
run out of oil 3. Will we use nuclear power
4. Will we travel to other planets 5. Will a lot
of people have test tube babies 6. Will people
still eat meat
*Numbers 7, 8 and 9 will be students' own
questions.*
3 1. I'll be there 2. He'll be here 3. I'll be there
4. He'll be there 5. She'll be here 6. it'll be
here

Unit Forty-One

1 1. Will you type it for me 2. Will you fix it for
me 3. Will you fix it for me 4. Will you do it
for me 5. Will you pick her up for me
2 1. I'll wash them for you 2. I'll do them for you
3. Bob'll (will) change it for you 4. Mary and I
will pick them up for you 5. Betty'll (will)
type it for you
3 1. will help 2. won't 3. won't 4. 'll 5. will help
6. won't 7. won't 8. 'll cut 9. will take 10. won't
11. 'll take 12. will help 13. will 14. 'll bake
15. will help 16. will 17. will 18. won't 19. won't
eat 20. 'll eat

Unit Forty-Two

1 1. d 2. a 3. b 4. f 5. g 6. e 7. c
2 1. might 2. might not 3. might 4. might
5. might not 6. might 7. might not 8. might

Unit Forty-Three

1 1. can't 2. can't 3. might not 4. can't 5. can't
6. might not 7. might not 8. can't
2 1. could 2. couldn't 3. couldn't 4. could 5. could
6. couldn't

Unit Forty-Four

1 1. must be 2. must be 3. must be 4. must not
be 5. must not
2 1. must be a fire 2. must not be in love 3. must
be planning to get married 4. must be on a
diet 5. must be a smoker
3 1. must be rich 2. must be on a diet 3. must
like 4. must have/dog 5. must be on fire (must
be burning)
There are many other possible answers.
4 1. She's wearing a ring./She must be married.
2. No one is answering the door./They must be
out. 3. I can't see the blackboard./I must need
new glasses. 4. I can't find their number in
the telephone book./They must not live here
anymore.

Unit Forty-Five

1 1. should quit smoking 2. should get more
exercise 3. should go back to school 4. should
stay where you are
2 1. should I do 2. Should I 3. Should I 4. Should
I 5. Should she 6. You shouldn't 7. you
shouldn't 8. ought
3 1. ought to 2. shouldn't 3. shouldn't
4. shouldn't 5. ought to 6. ought to

Unit Forty-Six

1 1. had better take 2. she'd (she had) better
slow down 3. had better start 4. had better
put out 5. had better stop
2 1. 'd better not 2. 'd better not 3. 'd better 4. 'd
better not 5. 'd better 6. 'd better

Unit Forty-Seven

1 1. must 2. must 3. mustn't 4. mustn't
5. mustn't 6. must
2 1. you mustn't 2. he doesn't have to 3. he
mustn't 4. he mustn't 5. you mustn't 6. you
don't have to 7. you don't have to

Unit Forty-Eight

1 1. Can 2. Can 3. won't 4. must 5. must 6. can't 7. might 8. can 9. might 10. should 11. ought to 12. Should 13. would you rather 14. 'll 15. will 16. should

2 1. may 2. should 3. Would you rather/would rather 4. will 5. Can/Can 6. must 7. Can/can

3 1. couldn't 2. can't 3. 'd rather not 4. shouldn't 5. might not 6. shouldn't

Unit Forty-Nine

1 1. are supposed to 2. am supposed to 3. are supposed to 4. are supposed to 5. isn't supposed to 6. aren't supposed to

2 1. what are we supposed to bring 2. Are we supposed to bring 3. 'm (am) supposed to bring 4. 's (is) supposed to bring 5. weren't supposed to bring 6. were supposed to bring

Unit Fifty

1 1. to get a good job. 2. to find someone to marry. 3. to please their parents. 4. to have a good time. 5. to get an education.

2 1. to start a new life 2. to find jobs 3. to provide for their families 4. to escape 5. to make money 6. to satisfy 7. to better their situation

Unit Fifty-One

1 1. how to get here 2. what to bring 3. how to type 4. where to send them 5. who to ask

2 1. I didn't know how to do it 2. I didn't know where to send them 3. She didn't know how many to buy 4. He didn't know which one to bring 5. I didn't know what to buy

3 1. how to manage 2. how to have 3. where to get 4. who to ask 5. how to accept 6. what to do 7. how to run 8. where to go

4 1. Do the instructions say what to do 2. Can you show me how to turn 3. Do you know where to go 4. Do you remember how long to cook the turkey 5. Does he know who to ask

Unit Fifty-Two

1 1. that he was 2. if he took 3. if he took 4. that he was 5. that he smoked 6. that he wore

2 1. whether my check came or not 2. whether Mary is coming to the party or not 3. whether I passed the course or not 4. whether I can use my credit cards or not

3 1. if there's a post office near here 2. if the buses run all night 3. if there's a place to wash clothes around here 4. if there's an inexpensive restaurant in the neighborhood 5. if there's a place to cash a check on Saturdays 6. if stores accept traveler's checks

4 1. whether she left last night 2. whether she came back early this morning 3. whether she came back 4. whether she took any luggage 5. that she took

Unit Fifty-Three

1 1. what his name is 2. where he lives 3. He doesn't know when the accident happened 4. He isn't sure how old he is 5. He didn't see who was driving the other car 6. He can't remember what he does for a living 7. He doesn't know whose fault it was

2 1. where you work 2. how long you have worked 3. how many loans you have already had 4. why you want the loan 5. how much money you earn 6. how old you are

3 1. Can you tell me where the post office is/Do you see where that man is standing/It's right behind him 2. Do you know how far the university is/I'm not sure how far it is 3. Do you know how often I have to make a payment/I'm not sure how often/Maybe twice a month

Unit Fifty-Four

1 1. used to be 2. used to do 3. making 4. wanted to become 5. being 6. getting to know 7. being 8. decided to move 9. leaving 10. becoming 11. starting

2 1. living 2. do 3. talking 4. change 5. eating 6. facing
Answers can be either Yes or No for each question.

3 1. meeting 2. making 3. getting 4. sailing 5. skydiving 6. hiking 7. parachute jumping 8. sitting 9. being 10. saying 11. hearing

4 1. used to 2. 'm used to 3. used to 4. 'm used to 5. 'm used to 6. used to 7. 'm not used to

Unit Fifty-Five

1 1. don't you 2. haven't I 3. isn't it 4. aren't I 5. don't I 6. didn't you 7. are you 8. have you 9. can't you 10. are you

2 1. c/aren't 2. d/is 3. b/didn't 4. e/don't 5. f/do 6. a/does

3 1. isn't it/it isn't/Florida 2. didn't it/it did/1962 3. does it/it doesn't/Saturn 4. aren't they/they are/Greece 5. don't they/they don't/caves 6. haven't they/they haven't/Venus

4 1. am I 2. haven't you 3. weren't they 4. could they

Unit Fifty-Six

1 1. ø 2. the 3. ø 4. the 5. the 6. ø 7. ø 8. the 9. ø 10. the

2 1. ø 2. a 3. the 4. a 5. the 6. the 7. ø 8. a 9. the 10. the 11. the 12. a 13. the 14. the

3 1. The/a/a star 2. The/the sun's 3. The/the/the/the Soviet Union/the

4 1. a 2. ø 3. ø 4. the 5. an 6. the 7. ø 8. a 9. The 10. The 11. ø 12. a 13. a 14. ø 15. a 16. The 17. ø 18. the 19. the 20. ø

Unit Fifty-Seven

1 1. looking forward to 2. checking into 3. waiting for 4. listening to 5. paying for 6. ran into (is running into) 7. laughing at 8. checking out of

2 1. paying for you 2. talk about it 3. ran into him 4. wait for it 5. think about her

3 1. get away from 2. run into 3. running out of it 4. cut down on 5. looking forward to it 6. look up to you

Unit Fifty-Eight

1 1. woke up 2. get up 3. move out 4. took off/picked up 5. moving in 6. cleaning up 7. calling up

2 1. Wake him up 2. Call her up 3. Figure it out 4. Turn it on 5. Call it off 6. Try them on 7. Put it out

3 1. found out 2. called her up 3. pick her up 4. try out 5. took it out 6. filled up 7. figure it out 8. break up

Unit Fifty-Nine

1 1. d/So do I 2. e/Neither do I 3. f/Neither does 4. a/So did I 5. b/Neither was 6. c/So should

2 1. so does Mary 2. neither does she 3. so are the people 4. neither are the heating bills 5. neither could my brother 6. neither did Mary

3 1. Jim hates to get up early, and so does Helen 2. Susan doesn't like to talk on the telephone, and neither do I 3. You should eat less, and so should I 4. I haven't been to Rio, and neither has Stan 5. I'd like to go to Hawaii this summer, and so would Martha

4 1. So are tigers 2. So have the Russians 3. So is England 4. So did the United States 5. So has Los Angeles 6. Neither do Venezuelans 7. So did Nigeria 8. Neither was Madame Curie 9. Neither has America

Unit Sixty

1 1. looked good 2. smelled sweet 3. looked beautiful 4. tasted delicious 5. felt energetic 6. sounded wonderful 7. looks ugly 8. look tired 9. looks worn out 10. feel depressed 11. sounds terrible 12. look better

2 1. beautifully/terrible 2. carefully/delicious 3. quietly/beautiful 4. hard/terrible 5. lovingly/sweet

3 1. looks unhappy 2. looks happy 3. smells delicious 4. smells sour 5. sounds wonderful 6. sounds horrible 7. tastes terrible 8. tastes delicious 9. looked horrible 10. looks (feels) fine

(continued)

4 1. They usually smell sweet 2. She (He) usually feels terrible (tired) 3. It usually smells sour (terrible) 4. It usually tastes sweet 5. They usually taste bitter (sour) 6. He (She) usually looks tired 7. They usually sound angry

Unit Sixty-One

1 1. one 2. another 3. another 4. the other 5. one 6. another 7. the other 8. the other 9. one 10. another 11. the other 12. one 13. one 14. Another 15. The other

2 1. the others 2. the other 3. the other 4. the other

3 1. Others 2. Others 3. other 4. others

4 1. another 2. each other 3. other 4. other 5. the other 6. each other

Unit Sixty-Two

1 1. What happened to your leg/How did you do it 2. Who lives in that ugly old house/Why does she live in such an ugly old place 3. Who took this picture/When did you take it

2 1. How far did you travel 2. How often do you see 3. What went wrong 4. Who does Mary live 5. When does the play start

3 1. How did he die 2. Who killed him 3. Who started it 4. When did it start 5. Who poisoned her 6. What did she eat 7. What time did she die 8. Who lived there 9. How long did they live there 10. What happened

4 1. Who discovered America 2. Who wrote *Romeo and Juliet* 3. How many feet are (are there) in a mile 4. When did the American Revolution begin 5. What is the capital of Honduras 6. How far is New York from Philadelphia 7. What destroyed Pompeii

Unit Sixty-Three

1 1. 've been 2. love 3. 've already been 4. went 5. 'll visit 6. 'll meet 7. 'll take 8. won't be 9. 'm having 10. haven't spent 11. 'll see

2 1. You did too 2. You weren't either/You were 3. She has too/She met him (They met) 4. I do too/I love you 5. He wasn't either/He was 6. I was too/I was

3 1. Was Kennedy president from 1952–1956/No 2. Does the U.S. president live in the White House/Yes 3. Did World War I last from 1914–1918/Yes 4. Has China been a member of the United Nations since 1973/Yes 5. Did the first men land on the moon in 1949/No 6. Was Nigeria a British colony/Yes 7. Have the Chinese been sending people into space for years/No

4 1. was 2. started 3. got up 4. had 5. started 6. was vacuuming 7. rang 8. answered 9. said 10. Is 11. said 12. has been 13. 'll be 14. said 15. jumped 16. drove 17. got 18. knew 19. got 20. found 21. were 22. was 23. called 24. reported

Notes

108